GERMAN SOC

RAYMOND ARON

GERMAN SOCIOLOGY

Translated by
Mary and Thomas Bottomore

THE FREE PRESS OF GLENCOE

German Sociology

Printed in the United States of America

FIRST FREE PRESS PAPERBACK EDITION 1964

For information, address:
The Free Press of Glencoe
A Division of The Macmillan Company
The Crowell-Collier Publishing Company
60 Fifth Avenue, New York, N.Y., 10011

Contents

Editor's Foreword

Professor Aron's *La Sociologie Allemande Contemporaine* was first published in 1936. By that date Hitler and the Nazis had already brought to an end the tradition of thought and enquiry which this book describes. Refugee scholars from the German lands contributed much to their new countries, but a chapter in the history of sociology was closed, and when free social enquiry and speculation became possible again in post-Nazi Germany even the prestige of such uncompromised scholars as L. v. Wiese or Alfred Weber could not re-open it. A new chapter was begun, and no one can as yet be certain either as to its content or its significance.

What is certain is the world-wide influence of the writers with whom this book is concerned. Yet, though they have been influential they have remained obscure. Translations and other expositions than this are available, yet, lacking the necessary philosophical clue they have, I think, been largely unsuccessful in the task of scientific communication for which they were intended. Professor Ginsberg in two compact essays, "The Problems and Methods of Sociology", and "Recent Tendencies in Sociology" which are to be found in his *Reason and Unreason in Society*,[1] Part I, alone in Britain fully possessed this clue. That Professor Aron grasps it these pages—and much else of his work—make abundantly clear.

In France, Britain and the United States of America the development of the social sciences has had an under-estimated but continuing unity. There has been a community of descent and of concern with similar problems and methods. In Germany the descent, the problems and methods of the social sciences, especially sociology, have only partly over-lapped with those of the world west of the Rhine. Philosophical problems and methods derived from Kant, an attitude to the data of history descended from Herder and Hegel, a dispute over the task and nature of economics found nowhere else in so extreme a form,

[1] London, 2nd ed., 1956.

and a continuing debate with Marx and Marxism, all combined to give classical German sociology its particular and separate character. These four themes form the background of this book.

As far as I know there is in English no recent history and exposition of German neo-Kantianism, but something of the immediate philosophical background to German sociology can be found in W. Brock, *Contemporary German Philosophy*[1] (Chapter I, and Chapter III, Part I). Professor Aron in his *La Philosophie Critique de l'Histoire*[2] has admirably discussed the second theme, while Professor Hodges' two books on Dilthey[3] treat lucidly of its major exemplar. The best short introduction to the relevant economic problems in English is probably the last selection of J. Schumpeter's *Economic Doctrine and Method* (London, 1954). There is, alas, no good book on Marxism and sociology—the writers who have attempted the task have usually known about one or the other, but not, with any justice and balance, about both. Mr. Bottomore and M. Rubel in their *Karl Marx: Selected Writings in Sociology and Social Philosophy*[4] have at least provided texts for the earlier part of Marx's life, but this is only a beginning. Passion and partiality still stand between us and just appraisal of Marx as sociologist, or of the protracted debate, implicit and explicit, which German sociologists have carried on with his shade.

This book, then, is important both as a chapter in the history of ideas and as a contribution to sociological theory. Despite the difficulties discussed above it is remarkably self-sufficient and I hope that it may prove in its English form useful to both lay and professional readers.

The present translation is based on the French second edition of 1950. The Appendix has been taken from the original text written for the 1953 German edition—*Die Deutsche Soziologie der Gegenwart* (Stuttgart, 1953). A small number of passages unlikely to interest English readers have been omitted. The bibliography is that of the German edition—the fullest which Professor Aron has provided.

DONALD G. MacRAE

[1] Cambridge, 1935.   [2] Paris, 2nd ed., 1950.
[3] *Wilhelm Dilthey*, London, 1944; *The Philosophy of Wilhelm Dilthey*, London, 1952
[4] London, 1956.

Introduction

German writers usually distinguish between nineteenth-century encyclopaedic sociology and the analytical sociology of the twentieth century. The sociology of Comte and Spencer was concerned with the whole history and social life of man. It was the culmination and synthesis of all the social sciences. At the same time historical and systematic, it determined laws and values and assimilated the human order to that of nature. It was in this form that sociology, arriving from France and England, was first known in Germany and, for the most part, rejected.

Until the beginning of this century, an independent sociology seems hardly to have existed in Germany. When M. Bouglé was studying the social sciences in 1895 he took as examples researches as diverse as those of Simmel on morals, Jhering on law, Lazarus and Steinthal on *Völkerpsychologie* and Wagner on economics. In other words, the social sciences were impregnated with the sociological spirit or method. Jurists and economists dealt tangentially with problems which today belong to sociology. (cf. 16,[1] p. 1 and *Spranger-Schmollers Jahrbuch*, vol. 49, 1925, p. 157.) Another factor which hindered the development of an independent sociology was the existence of a science of the state and of politics. But since the beginning of the century and especially since 1918, German writers have tried to create a distinct and autonomous science under the name of sociology.

It is true that some sociological work in the broader sense

[1] The first number in the references relates to the corresponding number in the bibliography.

(and perhaps the most interesting part) is still done by historians, jurists and economists. Economic theory and economic history are still imbued with the sociological spirit. Moreover, outside the general sociology which we shall mainly consider, there are several special sociologies (juridical, economic etc.). But whatever one may think of it, there does exist a distinct sociological literature, the more important works of which I should like to make known.

Analytical sociology has not adopted all the aims of encyclopaedic sociology; it is one social science among others and does not claim to interpret either the meaning or the values of human history. Moreover, it is divided into various parts. Formal sociology and historical sociology explore different areas; the one deals with the fundamental social relations, the types of social group, and the static structure of society, the other with the laws, or at least the theory, of the development of "bourgeois society".

There are also, undoubtedly, philosophical differences between the historical and the systematic schools. Does the essence of phenomena appear in concrete examples or in suprahistorical generalities? The historical school attaches most weight to culture and objective entities; the school of Simmel or of Vierkandt to human and, above all, social action. The same concepts may assume a different significance, according to the use made of them by one school or the other (cf. 121, pp. 245, 247). Social class, as conceived by historical sociology, is an almost metaphysical entity, situated at a certain point in history. Class, as defined by formal sociology, is a collection of individuals in the same condition (with the same income or the same way of life). But such an antithesis is by no means absolute, for the "class" of the philosophy of history should be empirically definable and should coincide with the analytical definition (even if, as in the work of Lukacs, it retains metaphysical privileges).

The best proof that these two schools are not separated by any insurmountable difference is furnished by the work of Max Weber. In fact we have not included Weber in any category, because he dominates all by his genius. His study *Über einige Kategorien der verstehenden Soziologie* and his analysis of the social framework in terms of individual action, belong to systematic sociology. His investigation of the relations between economics and religion brings him close to the historical and Marxist tradition. The sociologies of law, economics and religion (in *Wirtschaft und Gesellschaft*) appear to be "special sociologies", parts of a sociology both systematic and historical. In Weber's work there is not a simple juxtaposition but a genuine synthesis. His sociology of religion explains doctrines by social conditions, analyses the groups in which religions express and organise themselves, and investigates the influence of religious belief on human conduct.

Thus the themes and arrangement of this book may be outlined: first, systematic sociology, or to adopt the pleonasm gaining currency in the German vocabulary, sociology of society (*Gesellschaftssoziologie*), then historical sociology, and finally the work of Max Weber.[1]

[1] The size of this little book does not allow it to be exhaustive. I have omitted any discussion of Marxist sociology or of ethnography. I have not been able to give any account of Scheler, nor to mention the work of Koigen, Sander, Freyer, G. Salomon, and others.

CHAPTER I

Systematic Sociology

Sociology is the science of society. But this formula only poses the problem: what is society as distinct from the various realities, law, economics, the state, which are already studied by particular social sciences? Is society, considered as the union of these realities, anything but a fiction? Is there a science which directly studies the whole instead of analysing one of its aspects?

These questions seem to belong to the domain of methodology or of the theory of knowledge. In fact they belong to sociology; sociology, the youngest of the social sciences, is obliged to seek its subject matter and *this quest is an integral part of the science itself* (16, p. 16). Thus the preceding questions can be summarised in one question; what is social? What is the essence of every society, the common factor of innumerable instances?

Two answers are possible; in every group we see either relations between persons, or a distinct unity created by the collective life. The social *par excellence* can be understood either by the analysis of interpersonal events or by the intuition of wholes. Sociology, like philosophy, tends towards analysis or towards synthesis. A microscopic and macroscopic view are equally characteristic of the discipline, and Simmel and Spann represent the two extreme forms of the sociological viewpoint.

4

I. FORMAL SOCIOLOGY

Simmel[1] is rightly regarded as the founder of formal sociology which he conceived as a *geometry of the social world*. Just as geometry locates and measures relations in space, so sociology outlines the contours of a social universe which is usually hidden from us by our emotions and ideas. This form is the relation between individuals, considered apart from the objects represented or desired by these individuals. The same form appears in groups which pursue different ends, in periods remote from each other in time, while on the other hand, the same passions (revolutionary feeling for example), can develop in very different institutions. It would therefore be possible to separate form and content, and to distinguish abstract society, resulting from the interaction of individuals, from real society, created by men using the whole of their intelligence and feeling.

The social forms created by the "reciprocal action" (*Wechselwirkung*) of the members of a group can no doubt in the last analysis, be explained only by psychology. Let us consider, for example, the relations which arise when three people are in contact. We cannot understand the attitude of the *tertius gaudens*, or that of the *umpire*, without having recourse to psychological mechanisms. Moreover, the sociologist cannot predict the specific attitude which will be taken by a certain third party in a particular case. On the other hand, he can specify in advance all the possible relations into which three individuals, like three pawns on a chess board, are capable of entering. He must know the laws of behaviour of the pawns, in other words, the laws of human reaction. But he does not try to discover or to explain what goes on in the mind itself. He has a panoramic view of the lives of many individuals, under the categories of union or division, and his aim is to describe human groups and to analyse the processes through which society is created by

[1] Although Simmel does not strictly come within the period I am considering I thought it essential to devote a few pages to him. The development of sociology as an autonomous dicipline can, in fact, scarcely be explained without taking his work into account. It need hardly be said that the analysis which follows is very brief. Moreover, it is well known that sociology is only a part of Simmel's work in the social sciences. (In a more extensive study his *Philosophie des Geldes* and his conception of social psychology would have to be considered. Cf. *Archiv für Sozialwissenschaft und Sozialpolitik*, vol. 27.)

individuals, and individuals are moulded by the society they have made.

It would be impossible, and unnecessary, in the present context, to analyse Simmel's sociology. His work does not exactly correspond with the programme I have outlined and his analyses extend into the field of social psychology and philosophy. Moreover, his book, *Soziologie*, is by no means systematic; it is a collection of brilliant essays, the connection between which cannot always be seen, and which themselves lack unity and organisation. The reader becomes lost in an interminable succession, not so much of historical examples, as of theoretical cases and possible combinations. These dazzling exercises often seem like an elaborate game. The book has thus brought its author many admirers but few disciples.

What in fact is the main theme of Simmel's sociology? His chapter headings give sufficient indication; Quantitative Determination of the Group, The Forms of Authority and Subordination, Conflict, The Secret Society, The Intersection of Social Circles. In the study of hierarchy, Simmel examines the different forms of authority, varying according to whether it is exercised by one or several persons or by an objective power. He investigates the consequences of these different cases for the relations of the governed among themselves, of the governors among themselves, and for the relations between the governed and the governors; he also defines contrasting types: the independence allowed by submission to an impersonal power, and the subordination created by the presence of a leader. In other words the formal usually coincides with the general. In every society there are inequalities, and the sociology of the relations between individuals is at the same time the sociology of general phenomena or types.

Three classes of objection to Simmel's method can be distinguished:

(1) Those which concern the actual carrying out of the plan. These need not concern us here.

(2) Those which concern the basic concepts such as reciprocal action (a notion tainted with naturalism), form and content (always a relative opposition). Without discussing these criticisms, it should at least be noted that they leave intact Simmel's

basic aim, for the relations between individuals and the general characteristics of groups (leaving aside their economic and political aims etc.) certainly constitute a possible object of study.

(3) Those concerning the actual concept of the social which is implied by this scientific definition. Is the reality of social groups explained by identifying it with social relations, whose nature, spiritual or material, is itself left vague? Two schools in particular have criticized this identification: on the one hand, that of Spann, who, on the basis of his universalistic theory argues that if phenomena such as sympathy, suggestion, or gregarious instinct, are taken as the starting-point, it will never be possible to understand social facts such as war, power, or the state;[1] on the other hand, the school of sociologists imbued with a historical sense, who, though not questioning the legitimacy of a formal sociology, deny that the essence of the social can reside in suprahistorical relations of a general character.

Undoubtedly, Simmel would have rejected these criticisms, for his sociology has a philosophical foundation. In the first place, it is based on a theory of knowledge. The reduction of the whole to its elements is one of the theoretical principles of Simmel's method. Only those laws which regulate atomic movements are valid. A natural unity is defined by the reciprocal action of the parts. Thus sociology discovers individuals in the crowd.

Often, owing to our inability to resolve certain wholes into their elements, we must rest content with organising them by the use of concepts, as in history, when one speaks of "the battle of Marathon". In the same way, sociology does not concern itself with what takes place in men's minds, but with supra-individual realities, consituted with the help of the fundamental concepts —union and division.

Simmel's method is also based on a social philosophy. The dissolution of the idea of society as a real entity corresponds to a period in which the hostile classes are no longer united except by the fiction of one society. Crowds play a decisive role in democratic civilizations, and in the social sciences "the sociological spirit" expresses the individual's realization of the power

[1] 28, p. 27. Spann begins by positing that "the reciprocal action" of individuals is a psychological phenomenon.

of collectivities. Sociology as an autonomous science is an attempt to deal, by the method of positive science, with the perennial problem of the relations between the individual and the group, a problem which is especially prominent at the present time.

Finally, Simmel regarded crowds and institutions, not as superior beings, but as monstrous realities created blindly by men as a result of the collective life itself. In order to judge our civilization, he analyses human behaviour and men's relations with each other and with things. Thus Simmel's sociology expresses a double antimony, that between atomism and holism and that between individualism and the rule of the masses.

Von Wiese is the true continutor of Simmel, though he does not use the same expressions and entirely rejects the equivocal distinction between form and content. For the expression "reciprocal action" (which is almost always inaccurate since the influence of two individuals is never exactly reciprocal) he substitutes that of "reciprocal relation" (29, p. 84) (*Wechselbeziehung*), which is less open to criticism (for between master and pupil there exists a reciprocal relation even if all action is performed by the master on the pupil). But in spite of these external changes the central idea remains the same. It is still a matter of disregarding the cultural aims of individuals in society in order to study the influences which they exert on each other as a result of community life. The various social sciences analyse the ways in which men create law, the economic system and the state. Sociology studies the primordial conditions of culture and the milieu in which it is born; in other words, it studies society itself as it is formed and organized in the relations between individuals. Of course, this social sphere is never actually isolated in reality, but it is the sociologist's task to develop a special way of looking at things so that he always sees, even in the most complex and stable social forms, the uninterrupted basic movement of men approaching, withdrawing from, and influencing each other reciprocally. Thus one becomes aware of the very nature of the social, always present and always misunderstood.

The social sphere is a part of psychological reality, intermediary between the mental and the physical. The phenomena of approach and withdrawal studied by the sociologist are to a large extent psychological. But the sociologist does not describe their relationship to the individual consciousness as does the psychologist; he does not even consider the individual as complete in himself but analyses the effect of psychological phenomena both on the individual and on society. He studies the way in which the individual and the group are formed, and at the same time transformed, by the same social processes. Whereas these two terms are often opposed to each other as if they were two entities, one has only to go back to the formative process of each to dispose of this facile antinomy and to introduce the two inseparable methods, one starting from the whole and the other starting from the elements. Von Wiese considers the latter method somewhat superior, for the individual represents the primary reality which is immediately observable, while the group, as such, cannot be directly observed. But he does not deny the need for completing the analysis of elements by an understanding of wholes.

Von Wiese's theoretical programme is thus similar to that of Simmel, yet there are very great differences in their work. First, there is a contrast of scientific temperament. Von Wiese has attempted to construct a complete, harmonious and incontestable system. He wanted to show that it was possible to employ the same method everywhere and to analyse the whole of social reality with the aid of this method. He has therefore rejected the brilliant, improvised, supple analyses in which Simmel delighted and has sacrificed everything to considerations of scientific exactitude and a sort of "conceptual quantification".

The four fundamental concepts are those of social process,[1] distance, "social space" and social formation (*soziales Gebilde*). Two individuals meet in the street, greet each other and exchange a few words; and a social process has occurred. From the group formed by the witnesses of an accident to the group formed by the civil servants of a state or a post office, from temporary gatherings to permanent associations, sociology studies all phenomena from the same angle because they are essentially the same. In all cases it discovers social processes taking place in

---

[1] The relation is the result of the process statically considered.

social space (the area of social relations as distinct from physical space), bringing together or separating individuals (social distance is not to be confused either with physical distance or with the feeling of unity), creating social forms and crystallising or stabilising relationships which are at least real in their effects, since their presence in the consciousness of individuals, in the form of representations, determines the conduct of these individuals.

This analysis of processes results in a formula. The process (P) is the product of the behaviour of an individual (C) and the situation (S). Thus: $(P) = (C) \times (S)$.

But behaviour itself can be analysed: it is the product of temperament, of the ego,[1] as it is determined by heredity and the individual's experiences (E). On the other hand, the situation is a result of the natural environment (N) and the behaviour of others (C'). The latter in its turn can be analysed into hereditary factors (M') and experience (E'). Thus the definitive formula is:

$$(P) = (E) \times (N) \times (M') \times (E')$$

Any social process can be analysed completely by using this formula. Thus von Wiese leans towards behaviourism, not in the narrow sense of a materialist psychology which is not interested in phenomena of consciousness (in his sociological analysis von Wiese retains the act and its motive, behaviour and states of mind) but in the wider sense of social behaviourism; of how men behave in society.[2] Von Wiese's method is more positive and less psychological than that of Simmel.

This formula is the key to all von Wiese's investigations. It only remains for me to show how the system is built up. Social relations are of two kinds: individuals either draw nearer to each other or increase the distance between one another. (*zu und auseinauder*), either they are linked or they are detached (*binden und lösen*). *Tertium in sociologia non datur*. There is no third term; these two categories are exhaustive. Thus the first classification of simple processes is into those of approach and those of withdrawal (and, in addition, mixed processes which

[1] Sociology analyses the manifestations of the ego primarily in its social desires. Man wants: (1) security (2) esteem (3) the response of others (4) new experiences and sensations, (13, p. 169).

[2] 13, p. 147.

partake both of approach and withdrawal). Within the first category the processes are distinguished in terms of the degree of proximity which they establish between individuals, from simple contact (I ask a passer-by the time) to union, passing through approach, adaptation and assimilation. Contact (two witnesses of the same accident) may lead to conflict as well as to union (they see the event differently).[1] The essential inter- mediate stages here are competition and conflict.

The second part of the book is devoted to the theory of forma- tions. The principle of the classification of formations is as follows: how far away does the individual conceive the whole?[2] The mass which emerges at the circus or the theatre, or in the street, is felt by the individual to be very near: thus he is directly aware that though it determines him it does not com- pletely escape from the action he exerts on it. Further away is the group (a club, a body of civil servants), distinguished from the mass by its duration and relative continuity which shows at least an embryonic organisation. The members of the group build up a representation of the whole, then traditions and cus- toms are born, as well as relations between the groups, and finally, within each of them, a model is suggested to all the members as an ideal (29, p. 496). In the third place the social bodies (*Körperschaften*) or abstract collectivities result from the accumulation of simple formations. They derive only indirectly from social processes, but this does not mean that we have to abandon the "relational" principle, for social constraints and the influence of the state, the people or the church, or the individual, bring us back to the action of all men, past or present, on a single person (29, p. 509). Social bodies are born of groups when there is a representation of the unity of the whole and a will to make it endure (29, p. 520). Thus they imply (29, p. 524) (1) an ideal and a moral code, (2) a technical organization of relations of individuals among themselves and with things. The social body always bears the mark of human passions, for it is men who have blindly created these collective beings which determine their lives. The most typical social body is the state

---

[1] Of course this example is only an illustration; violent conflicts generally develop within formations.

[2] 13, pp. 402–3.

(other examples are church, class, and economic system). It derives from men's will either to ensure order, power and security, or to perpetuate ideal values. Social bodies are neither worse nor better than the men of whom they are the product and the reflection.

In the first part of his system, von Wiese analyses not only simple processes of approach and withdrawal but also the complex processes which arise only within formations. Processes of approach are those by which individuals are made uniform, assigned to their social positions, socialised, etc. Processes of withdrawal are those which give rise to inequalities, masters and servants (*herrschen und dienen*), a hierarchy, classes, selection, exploitation etc. The analysis of social bodies then follows strictly the rules of the method; this requires us to pay attention, not indiscriminately to all the many problems raised by the social bodies, but only to the central problem: what particular processes determine the character of the social body under consideration? In the same way, we can apply the principle of bipolar consideration—to study how the individual determines the group and the group the individual. The formula of analysis is also implicitly used. To understand a social body is to understand the human desires which created it (M) and the obstacles which had to be surmounted (N) or (C'). (In the case of the state, it is to surmount the obstacle to communal life which results from the clash of wills to power).

Of course, von Wiese's aim is not entirely realised by such a system. The latter is merely intended to show the fertility and legitimacy of sociology conceived in this way, to suggest a viewpoint and to provide a method and a body of concepts. Moreover, von Wiese himself tries to apply his method to concrete problems; in particular he has studied the village[1] as a social formation. "Relational" sociology will become more useful as it helps to solve more problems and as more special sociologies are added to general sociology.

The logical coherence of the method cannot be doubted. The *sociology of relations* is a method which can be used. Nevertheless,

---

[1] *Ergänzungsheft zu den Kölner Vierteljahresheften für Sociologie. Das Dorf als soziales Gebilde.* Munich 1928. Cf. also in vol. viii of the same journal the article of W. Latten, and in vol. x that of Gierlichs.

a certain lack of clarity remains. In the first place, the fundamental concepts seem rather obscure, expecially that of distance. Although von Wiese tries to make the notion clearer (29, p. 122) and although he asserts that distance is intuitively and immediately apprehended, I still find the concept difficult to grasp. I visualise it as a complex impression, resulting from the material situation and affective impressions together, rather than as something simple.

The same difficulty reappears in the definition of the subject matter of sociology, which is conceived as both physical and moral. A social fact is neither the physical fact of a handshake, nor the motive of the action, but the two things at once. Consequently, sociology belongs neither to the category of psychology nor to that of natural science; it occupies an intermediate position. Undoubtedly, such an attitude can easily be justified if one is simply seeking a method. But, in the eyes of those sociologists who are trying to provide a philosophical basis for sociology, this compromise seems tainted either by naturalism or by individualism or with abstract theorizing.

On the other hand, von Wiese's conception is based primarily on a definite philosophy of the social, on a reduction of the essence of society to interpersonal relations. If the notion of social distance and the sphere of the social are not intuitively apparent, or if they are not defined with complete precision, this sociology can only be justified by its fertility. The theoretical system, however rigorous, does not prove that the method of observation applied to reality gives the most fertile results. It seems that such a science is more descriptive than explanatory. It describes, groups and classifies various social processes, but in order to explain them it would be necessary to go beneath the social to biological facts, or beyond social phenomena to the psychological or spiritual sphere. Undoubtedly, though von Wiese limits the social in relation to the biological and the spiritual, he makes use of the laws of biology and psychology. But it may be asked whether sociology does not have to go beyond this restricted sphere if it is to explain social relations, and consequently whether it is not obliged to choose between remaining purely descriptive or trespassing beyond these limits.

Was it, then, really useful to construct a system? While

awaiting the genuine quantification of which von Wiese dreams, is this kind of conceptual quantification of relations fruitful in a world of pure qualities? Does the infinite diversity of distances indicated by the innumerable concepts provide a better understanding, or will it help us in the future to a better understanding of collective life?

Finally, the essential question remains. Should formal sociology seek to isolate itself increasingly as one independent discipline among others? Or should it, on the contrary, aim at becoming the fundamental science for all the social sciences?

II. Society and Community

Although Tönnies' famous book *Gemeinschaft und Gesellschaft*[1] appeared in 1887, it deserves mention in a study of contemporary sociology. The book is too well known to require a long analysis, but it may be of some value to recall its basic aim. It was the result of prolonged reflection upon the philosophy of Hobbes, natural law and socialism.[2] Men in *society* are those described in Hobbes' *Leviathan* (40, p. 122). The distinction between society and community transcends the opposition, which is traditional in the philosophy of law, between the natural and the artificial. There exist two kinds of human grouping, one on the model of the living organism, the other analogous to a constructed machine, but each is as natural as the other, since the second derives from the first by an inevitable process. The profound solidarity born of common feeling manifested in the family, inevitably disappears in the interest of an external juridical order when the division of property and the opposition of interests separates the members of the group. So-called natural law, based on the equality of individuals, is only the idealization of civil law, that of merchants and property

---

[1] This book is only a part of Tönnies' work. Among his more important books should be mentioned: *Kritik der öffentlichen Meinung*, Berlin, 1922; *Soziologische Studien und Kritiken, I, II, III*, Iena, 1925, 1926, 1929; and *Einführung in die Soziologie*, Stuttgart, 1931. This last work outlines a pure sociology (which, in Tönnies' system, comes after general sociology—social biology and social psychology—and before applied sociology). The antithesis of *society* and *community* (like that of authority and cooperation) plays the role of fundamental modes of all social beings, the proper subject matter of sociology. According to their degree of unity, these social beings are relations, wholes or organisms. The theory ends with a study of values, norms and systems (*Bezugsgebilde*)

[2] Marxism is used especially in the analysis of economic society.

owners, which, far from being primitive, is born of the dissolution of the community.

The book was not only concerned to resolve a problem of legal philosophy, but also tried to establish the bases of a pure sociology and to outline a comparative history of cultures. In fact, the opposition of the two social types is explicable in the last analysis by the distinction between two forms of human will on the one hand, the *Wesenswille*, a profound, organic will, an expression of nature itself, which determines means and ends indissolubly related according to experienced pleasures as they result from spontaneity, habit and memory, and on the other hand, the *Kürwille*, will as decision, which is characterized by reflection and which starts from an abstractly conceived end in order to determine the technically most appropriate means. On the one hand the solidarity of organ and function, on the other hand the liberty of judgment. If this psychological distinction is the basis of sociological theory, we can formulate the following principle of method: to understand human groups is to relate them to the will of the men who create the collectivity.

These two concepts not only have numerous applications in reality, they not only make precise and stylize the distinction between the two sexes,[1] between the masses and educated men,[2] between domestic work and commerce; they also represent in a pure form the two extreme terms of a historical development now drawing to a close and which once led to the decay of the Roman Empire. On the one side (40, p. 247) there is family life ruled by simple feeling, village life regulated by custom, and even city life where religion still binds men together; on the other, there is the life of large towns where individuals give free rein to their desire for profit and power, politics which oscillate between the demand for individual liberty and the despotism of the state, and finally, going beyond the boundaries of real communities, a cosmopolitan life, a public opinion and a republic of educated people extending to all parts of the world. But this triumph of *society*, in spite of the values thus created, is not without danger for communal life; all the fundamental bonds are destroyed, and the people die of this hypertrophy resulting from an urban and commercial existence. The process

[1] *Einführung*, p. 265 and 40, pp. 144–45.   [2] 40, pp. 152–53.

of drawing together in space ends by eliminating union in time. Excessive development of the intelligence leads to diminished vitality and to misconceptions of the conditions of existence adapted to the environment. Socialism and the class struggle correspond to *society* in its last stage, dissolving the last organic ties, objectivising all wealth and bringing it into rapid circulation; leaving only men ruled by their own caprice, without scruple, faith, constancy or religion. Socialism is both the expression of this *society* and the demand for complete state regulation; consequently it tends to destroy the anarchical society from which it derives.

In spite of, or perhaps because of, its wealth of material, the book remained almost unknown for many years. The second edition appeared in 1912 and there have been many subsequent editions. There are scientific and political reasons for this success after so long a silence. Until the beginning of the century, there was hardly any independent sociology in Germany. But since the first years of this century and especially since the 1914-18 war, sociology has increasingly developed as an autonomous science. Now Tönnies' book *was* pure sociology. It used concepts closely approaching Max Weber's ideal type. The phenomenologists too could find in it concepts of essence. The explanation of collectivities by the will of their members constitutes a possible basis for a theory of groups. Finally, these two concepts (*community* and *society*) had both a historical and a supra-historical meaning; they referred to the basic structure of societies and also to different periods of social development.

Nevertheless, all these reasons would not suffice to explain the rôle that this antithesis has played, and still plays, in German sociology. These two concepts are in fact characteristic of a great part of German sociology and social philosophy. And there is no better demonstration of the involvement of all sociology in social reality. The opposition of *society* and *community* constitutes one of the central themes of the science, because it also contributes to German political ideologies. The reaction[1] against

---

[1] The equivocal nature of the community ideology is not, of course, responsible for political events. It is just that this ideology explains how and why popular indignation has turned against non-community ways of thinking and against republicanism and liberalism considered as characteristic of *society* and responsible for its miseries.

mechanistic civilization and against an abstract social order has taken the return to "community" as its watchword. It must be recognised that this word, which is rarely used in political discourse in France, has to German ears the same sound as our "justice and equality". All the revolutionary movements against contemporary society in Germany aim at the same ideal of solidarity of feeling, of real unity and harmony with nature. They attack the same enemies—the individualism of economic man, the rivalry of various interests, brutal competition, and the inhuman organization created by law, by convention or by economic processes. All these vague aspirations crystallize round two antitheses: those of culture and civilization which I shall study later, and those of society and community. A youth movement, like National Socialism, invoked the idea of an authentic community. Animated by a horror of discipline, formalism, and artificiality, the movement has transformed the lives and minds of many young people. National Socialism, in spite of the enthusiasm and faith of its adherents has, by a tragic paradox, contributed to the creation of an order more tyrannical than that which it wished to destroy.

In spite of his preference for the community, Tönnies would hardly recognize his doctrine either in this political movement or even in cultural romanticism. In any case, he intended to remain a scholar, not to become a prophet or a demagogue. Nevertheless, the political confusion has its counterpart in a scientific ambiguity. There is, first, an ambiguity as to value: Tönnies, like many German sociologists, suggests, though perhaps without intending to do so, the superior value of the community.[1] He prefers the affective to the rational, organic harmony to legal order. There is also an ambiguity as to meaning : can the two types have both a theoretical and non-historical bearing? By dint of giving them several meanings, does not Tönnies end by multiplying the uncertainties? Is the antithesis exhaustive?

It would take too long and would in fact be without much interest to follow the development of Tönnies' theory in socio-

---

[1] Tönnies declares his impartiality. Cf. *Einführung* VI–VII. Undoubtedly his ideal is not the return to a primitive community, but the transformation of society by true socialism.

logical literature. It can be found, explicitly or implicitly, in nearly every writer. There is a resumé of its various possible forms in Leemans' book (41) and in an article in the Dictionary of Sociology (11). I shall mention here only one of Tönnies' followers.

In an admirable article (42, pp. 35-105), Schmalenbach has contrasted the community as a natural union, with the federation (*Bund*) as a harmony of feeling or enthusiasm. The one is based on blood ties or communal life and is spiritual and unconscious; individuals are only aware of it when it is threatened. The other is born of a sudden agreement, a renewal, a collective emotion. The Church is a community, the sect is a federation. The one belongs to everyday life, and is exemplified by the family; the other arises from exceptional circumstances, such as friendship. The concept of federation enables us to understand certain primitive forms of religious life as well as the youth movement or National Socialism: unity in faith, in the revolt against family or society, in love for the leader. None of these groups have anything in common either with blood ties or with the cold rationality of legal agreements. There is no doubt that the phenomena of German social life had as large a part as the ethnological discovery of federations of men (*Männerbund*) in suggesting this new category to Schmalenbach.

This distinction makes the use of Tönnies' categories more fruitful, as is shown by the correspondence between the three essential categories of the political sociology of Max Weber— rational power (bureaucratic), traditional power, charismatic power—and the three concepts of society, community and federation (legal, familial and friendship relations, 42, p. 98).

Moreover, it becomes quite clear that these concepts only have a scientific value when they refer, not to specific groups (nobility, bourgeoisie, etc.) but to different modes of existence of all groups (42, p. 79). Undoubtedly a certain period may have a greater affinity for some particular mode, as for example, the present time has for the societal. It does not follow from this that our social life is pure *society* and consequently condemned to decay.

Finally, it becomes possible to raise in a more precise way the problem of the historical and logical types of these three social forms. Clearly, the development to which Tönnies gave most attention, the dissolution of community into *society*, is *one* typical development. But the relation of these forms is more complex. There is hardly any community which does not already show traces of *society*. At the beginning of the societal order, there is often enthusiasm and heroism, just as the family community extends the federation founded on personal love. Any federation, if it is to endure, must substitute fidelity for love; that is, a precise undertaking to be absolutely faithful. Friendship must become apparent as in the family or must be organized as *society*. The legal order assumes at first a communal agreement, but, when the unconscious unity is loosened, legal ties become indispensable unless enthusiasm leads to the birth of a new community.

Perhaps the political significance of these terms will be less obscure if stated thus: in the heat of revolution, full of the spirit of federation, young people desire a communion which they call community. But the passion is appeased and a legal order is again essential. Thus the problem is plainly posed: is a spiritual revolt, which is by nature exceptional and temporary, enough to transform society, or rather, in what circumstances is such a revolt capable of producing a true community or a new organization?

III. Phenomenological Sociology

Vierkandt may be considered a disciple of Simmel as well as of Tönnies. The two directions of systematic sociology which we have just distinguished both lead to his system. The latter could, then, be provisionally defined as an attempt to combine formal sociology, which studies the relations between individuals, and the sociology of Tönnies, which analyses the types of social groups and social beings.

Vierkandt adopts an intermediate position between individualism and universalism. According to Simmel, the unity of the whole can be reduced to the reciprocal action of its elements. The reality of the whole, on the contrary, is both logically and empirically the basic datum in the philosophy of Spann. Neither of these two formulations corresponds to Vierkandt's conception. He tries to correct each by the other, to discover the reality of the whole *within* individuals, and to use a double method of analysis (of the parts and of the whole). He combines the collective consciousness of Durkheim (or Litt's group-mind)[1] with Simmel's formalism.

In the first edition of his book, there is, indeed, the impression of a simple juxtaposition. Chapter I (46 (1st ed.), p. 47-53) is concerned with the dissolution of all ideas of substance, and with the reduction of all social unities to functions. The concept of relation is taken as fundamental for all sociology, because the relation between individuals constitutes the primary process of every society. In the fifth chapter, on the other hand, there is a study of *objective forms* (personal or supra-personal) of the collective mind, and of the specific causality of the group. The analysis of social impulses, and the adoption of the *society*-community antithesis did not apparently facilitate the passage from formal analysis to the apprehension of wholes.

The second edition of the book undoubtedly marks an advance towards integration. Formalism yields increasingly to the intuition of totalities. Tönnies' contrast is made less rigid; there is no *society* devoid of all community, there are only forms more or less close to the primitive community. The fundamental relations are mixed in real life. Finally, the phenomenological method is used in a more precise and deliberate way; the intention is to lead to the synthesis of the two theories which we have distinguished.

The phenomenological method is not in this connection opposed to psychology. On the contrary, the point of departure of the theory remains, viz. social psychology, regarded as the study of the social conduct of men (i.e. of their conduct with reference to other men). The analysis goes back to the fundamental social dispositions because their effectiveness presupposes a common life. But these dispositions are sufficiently plastic to change in the course of history. Man is a historical being, the product of collective forces which mould him in each epoch; he has no existence prior to that of society. Natural man is only a utopian ideal (or a legitimate abstraction) never to be found in real life, even in primitive groups.[2]

---

[1] Cf. *Individuum und Gemeinschaft*, 3rd edition, Leipzig and Berlin, 1926.
[2] Cf. 46 (1st ed.), pp. 25-7.

In this way the question of priority between sociology and psychology is avoided. Individual differences clearly result from historical events, and the individual is always formed by the group. But it is not impossible to discover the constants of human nature in all the various appearances of man in history. The social dispositions[1] with which psychology deals are therefore primary in two different senses; they are innate, and they are the common root of all the tendencies which can be observed in various societies. And since these dispositions are ultimately apprehended by a phenomenological intuition which ensures their irreducible character, perhaps one should add a third sense, and call them also *a priori*, as being part of the very essence of man.

Examples of the essential dispositions are self-awareness (*Selbstgefühl*, cf. 46 (1st ed.), pp. 60-68 and 4, pp. 546-48), the instinct of submission (*Unterordnungstrieb*), the tendency to give help, to receive ideas, beliefs and sentiments (which branch into autonomous phenomena, suggestion, sympathy, etc.). Let us consider the instinct of submission (cf. 46 (1st ed.), pp. 68-97 and 11, pp. 549-52). Naturalism would try to reduce all obedience to fear or self-interest, fear of punishment or hope of reward. In fact, we submit spontaneously before the being who imposes obedience. Any explanation in terms of association of ideas would falsify the authentic reality of the sentiment. We are dealing with an ultimate fact which cannot be broken down into simpler elements; men are so constituted that they obey the individual whose personality seems to them to have value. The internal imitation of the master by the disciple, an expression of respectful admiration, has nothing in common with the external imitation brought about by opportunism or the desire to conform. Authority is a spiritual phenomenon, anterior to class differences and the power of institutions. The superior being directly imposes himself on other people.

Similarly, the satisfaction one feels in being recognised by others (*Anerkennung*) derives from a deep-seated instinct. The esteem of others is desired, not for the advantages it brings or the difficulties which it removes, but for itself. Man speaks

[1] Vierkandt designates by this term ways of thinking and feeling as well as of acting.

directly to man. The "values" at which we aim are originally
derived from the judgments of our group, the arbiter of good
and evil in closed and integrated societies. But the group is also
the source of morality; we judge ourselves from the point of
view of other people in order to gain the approval of the
spectator. Sometimes we even substitute for the real group an
ideal group of which our individual conscience may seem to us
to be the authentic interpreter. Heteronomy consists in accepting the judgment, not of a close and living collectivity, but of
the world or of "other people". Thus self-awareness ramifies
into the desire for authority and value, into pride, etc.

The bonds which unite individuals are thus internal in a
double sense. They bind them together directly, without the
medium of bodily movement or the intervention of conscious
thought. They are born of respect and love, not of fear and
utility. Starting from these initial facts, society (cf. 11 pp. 560-
562) as a general term, is easily defined, since the individual, far
from being enclosed within himself, participates in the life of
other people and derives from others not only his ideas, affec-
tions and desires but the awareness of himself. The essence of
social life implies a certain minimum of reciprocity (cf. 11,
p. 163), the reaction of man to man, and the expansion of the
ego beyond its own limits. The individual consciousness is
primarily "outside itself". Such a phenomenon will always
remain incomprehensible to the naturalist who wants to subject
spiritual relations to the logic of things. It is, on the other hand,
immediately obvious to anyone who is willing to observe his
own experience without prejudice and to judge it intuitively.

If this internal bond is the fundamental characteristic of any
society, the community must be its ideal form. Only in a community do all the social dispositions flourish; unity, without
being complete, is here both spiritual and intellectual. It is born
of love, of devotion and of the desire to help one another and,
at the same time, it consists of a common affirmation of order;
it is the enduring feeling of individuals that they constitute a
whole.

The community enjoys a priority both systematic and historical. It comes first because it is the full realization of social
life, and it is first in time because a union of souls must always

be the basis on which less passionate and more intellectual relations are established. There is no longer any agreement of minds in those social forms which diverge greatly from the community. The social act in a legal relationship consists in the statement of a similar meaning, not in direct agreement. In conflict and in power relations the divergence is still greater. Opposing values are affirmed; in the first case there is an attempt to wound, in the second case there is separation into classes of whom some exercise power and others have only to obey.

Nevertheless, in all these examples there remain social feelings. The two partners in an exchange do not perform isolated actions. As parties to an action which they know they are performing together, each wishes to respect the law and the other partner and to feel confidence in the other. In warfare, there are rules which must not be broken. There are definite limits to what one has to fear. Moreover, adversaries often feel bound not only by the code of war they are observing, but by an anterior solidarity. They want to defeat each other, precisely because their wills are opposed and because they feel their community in the same conflict. Finally, the power of an upper class is neither absolute nor arbitrary, and the obedience of a lower class is not always forced, nor always contrary to the interests of the subjects. In all these relationships different moralities hold sway, appropriate to the character of these various ways of life (and in reality always more or less mingled). Beyond the sphere of power society disappears, and there remain only relations between things, with no trace of reciprocity; man encounters inanimate objects which he uses or destroys. Hence the merciless war against savages, slavery, and certain modern forms of enterprise where the minimum of internal community has disappeared.

The theory of fundamental relationships passes without any break in continuity to the theory of the group, for the same social manifestations are seen in the group and explain its cohesion. Although it has its own life and internal unity (11, pp. 241-44) the group lives in individuals and not outside them.

Each group is characterized by a "spirit" which constitutes an individuality (the spirit of a regiment, of a town, of a country, the Prussian spirit). The spirit outlives generations and has the continuity and permanence in time of a collective being. Nevertheless nothing in this phenomenon goes beyond the sphere of observable facts. Each individual is moulded by the group, because he receives directly from his surroundings the instrument of his thought and his standard of values.

The individual experiences the group as an entity both superior to, and born in, all men. If he recognises the other person as a friend it is through the collectivity present in everyone, but the group in its turn depends on individuals (as conditions, not as causes). If the flux of community experienced in the individual consciousness comes to an end, the group disappears.

Moreover, the group has an internal unity, and individuals spontaneously divide their lives into two parts, that which concerns the collectivity and that which concerns only themselves. No matter how far back in history one goes, this distinction will be found. The nearer one approaches to primitive communities, the larger is the place of the collective consciousness in the minds of individuals, and the more powerful and spontaneous it is. This is not simply to say that the individuals are less unlike one another than in modern society, that they are more alike in their feelings and ideas. It is to say also that they attach a social meaning to a greater number of their actions, and that they more frequently regard themselves as members of a group and not as private persons. Thus it is possible to speak of the group's will to live, of a collective consciousness, a *real* but not *substantial* unity, in and through individuals. Thus, also, it is possible to distinguish the tribal spirit from the individualist spirit, according to whether the individual is primarily a member of the collectivity or is autonomous (collective or individual responsibility, national religion or a religion of personal salvation).

The group life is always regulated by a system of rules (cf. 11, pp. 249-51) (custom, mores, morality, law) which constrains all the members. These rules, originating from social life, have as their object the maintenance of its unity. Impersonal and objective formations (institutions, monuments, languages, mores, morality, ritual) develop a force of their own and contribute to maintaining the collectivity in existence.

The unity of the group is therefore neither absolute nor transcendent; it is the product of the ordered diversity of individual existences, of vanquished oppositions, and even of organised conflicts. It has an internal structure and it may be more or less complete at different times (for example, when the group is in conflict with other groups, there is likely to be increased awareness of unity). This unity is, above all, the product of a definite chain of causes, and of the field of action which it constitutes, which has its own laws.

Systematic sociology is immersed in and penetrated by historical conceptions. Vierkandt was an ethnologist before he turned to philosophical sociology, and his sociological theory retains certain elements of a philosophy of history. The theory is founded upon a distinction between two types of society: one, the close-knit primitive communities in which there are neither classes nor a social hierarchy, where the tribal spirit is strongly developed and where co-operation (*Genossenschaft*) is dominant; and the other, our modern societies which are divided into hostile classes and in which every individual is primarily his own master. The distinction between tribal morality (11, pp. 245-47 and 192-93) and individualist morality, as well as the theory of the basic social relations, represents a transposition of certain notions of historical evolution (or, let us say, these notions retain a historical as well as a systematic value). Vierkandt also takes up the notion of collective causality, suggested, apparently, by historical researches.[1] Finally, he discusses examples in social reality of the forms which he has analysed theoretically. Thus the last part of the book is devoted to historical examples of social groups (the family and the state).

Phenomenology is intended, as we have seen, to aid the systematization of these notions, which are drawn from diverse sources. It has been used in practice in the following ways:

(1) To abstract the pure types by intuition, without having recourse to generalization from individual instances. It is in this way that community, the very essence of social life, is defined.

(2) To apprehend directly the basic sentiments. For example, submissiveness, or the experience of the group, are presented as ultimate data.

---

[1] Cf. *Die Stetigkeit im Kulturleben*, Leipzig, 1908.

(3) To distinguish the different meanings of attitudes which externally resemble each other. For example, obedience may be expressed in the same gestures, whether it is the result of love, of self-interest, or of fear.

(4) To apply a non-spatial logic to the spiritual phenomena of social life. Conversation is not simply a communication of ideas, still less an exchange of words. Its essence is the direct contact between persons; the purpose of the discussion is less important that the silent language which the individuals speak to each other with their whole being. Here again Vierkandt calls upon phenomenology as an aid to understanding the hidden meaning of these spiritual relations, and he opposes the phenomenological method to a logic which would not go beyond the persons and sensible objects. In the same way the expansion of the self which occurs in any community calls for a phenomenological method.

(5) To apprehend totalities as such, rather than to construct them from their elements. This "holistic" method is opposed to that of summative consideration (*summative Betrachtung*) and is employed especially in order to posit the unity of the group or of objective formations. (Such a procedure is only phenomenological if the totality in question is incapable of analysis.)[1]

It is an undeniable merit of Vierkandt's book and of the method he adopts that it tends towards pure description. In this sense we recognise the value of point no. 3. But it should be noted that all we are concerned with here is a phenomenological psychology (not a transcendental phenomenology) in the broad sense in which it becomes identical or almost identical with sympathetic intuition. We can give the same meaning to the pretentious and bizarre formulations of a non-spatial logic. The latter, in reality, is opposed only to a popular associationist or naturalistic psychology. The facts grouped under the heading of "expansion of the self" are not new. It has long been known that one can suffer in the sufferings of others and be happy in their happiness, without any egoistic reflex. Just as the spatial formula of "expansion" must not be literally interpreted, so also discussion has never been interpreted as the

---

[1] Vierkandt does, in fact, analyse these totalities.

transmission of speech from one place to another. It is a matter of pure description of spiritual phenomena.

As to the "essential types", the "ultimate facts", and the "directly intuited wholes", they contain many obscurities. Max Weber's method of ideal types is legitimate; phenomenology there serves only to establish the types as essences. Is this claim justified in the case of Vierkandt's concepts? In what sense is a disposition such as submissiveness a fundamental datum?

Let us note that psychological analyses do not permit an "explanation" of social phenomena; social dispositions are extracted from social life before being used to give an account of it. If the procedure were put forward as explanatory it would involve a vicious circle. We are concerned once again with pure description. Why is submissiveness an ultimate fact? Because it is innate? Phenomenology has no concern with a quality of this kind. Or because it cannot be reduced to a combination of more simple sentiments? In this case we are referring to a unique mode of behaviour, and we revert to a phenomenological psychology.

Is the ideal type of a society based on "inner bonds" essential? To reply to this question a thorough critical examination of the theory of fundamental social relations would be necessary. Let us note the ambiguity of such expressions as "inner bond" (spiritual or moral bond), warmth or coldness, closeness or remoteness of social relations. Moreover, the general definition of society as an expansion of the self involves the exclusion from "social life" of forms of social life in which the vestiges of the sentiment which still upholds them have disappeared (if conformity with the rules arises from purely utilitarian considerations). It would exclude unregulated warfare, slavery, and certain types of industrial work. This is a strange essence which tends to disappear, or completely disappears, in certain phenomena which manifestly belong to the field of observation. It would be better to present this definition as an ideal type, as one possibility among others.

As to the totalities, phenomenological intuition is much less useful in apprehending them as such than in facilitating their analysis (which does not mean their reduction to other elements). Vierkandt himself analyses collective phenomena by a continual shifting of perspective between the elements and the whole. Phenomenology here serves to affirm the reality of the group as such. But it is precisely this reality which remains vague. "Collective causality" or "complex of action" (*Wirkungszusammenhang*) are ambiguous expressions, and the former has a naturalistic character. One arrives eventually at such formulae as the "creative character of spiritual relations". Thus there is an oscillation between psychological and "holistic" formulae.

These remarks are not intended to present a detailed criticism but to draw attention to some difficult points. They are not intended to minimise the value of these very subtle psychological analyses, but to show the gap between a phenomenological social philosophy and this type of sociology which makes use of a psychology largely derived from the ideas of Husserl, and finally to emphasise the predominance in this theory of the notion of community which is the transposition of an emotional preference.

IV. Universalistic Sociology

It is difficult to give Professor Spann his due. He has already published an impressive amount of scholarly work. He is the leader of a school, followed by enthusiastic disciples and attacked by violent critics. It may be said that he himself incites a somewhat brutal criticism by his imperious demand that one should take sides and by the way in which he introduces emotional passions into scientific questions by the insertion of political and value judgments. Thus anyone (like myself) who finds the atmosphere of universalism uncongenial is tempted to see in his lengthy books, words, literary talent and religious feeling, rather than philosophical rigour or contributions to knowledge.

According to Spann the antinomy between individualism and universalism is decisive for the theory of the social sciences. This fundamental antinomy appears in a varity of different forms, and it may be expressed in the following way. Either the individual exists in himself, completely formed and self-sufficient, in which case he receives nothing from outside himself except mechanically-transmitted knowledge; he can experience a constraint which informs or deforms him, but if he succeeds in realising his nature he owes nothing to others. Or, on the other hand, the individual is not autonomous, he exists only in and through the community, and can be understood only as an element in a whole, as an organ of a superior being. In this case, universalism is true. Science and morality will be different according to which of these principles is chosen. In the one case, the moral ideal is that of the hero (51, p. 59) who resists the world's assault and is victorious through his own strength. In the other, the ideal is that of the sage or the saint; a community of man, the world, and God. In one case, logical and moral relativism, utilitarianism and empiricism will be preferred; in the other, certain knowledge of absolutes, the reality of spirit and of God.

For science, and above all for the social sciences, the choice between these alternatives is decisive. And according to Spann, the choice can be based upon observation of reality, independently of metaphysical presuppositions. Individualism begins its analysis of society with individuals. It finds its true expression in the theory of contract or of natural law, and it leads to anarchy or to Machiavellianism. Moreover, it tries to reduce society to the reciprocal relations of individuals, an obscure and inadequate notion. Thus it looks in vain for causal relations whereas social reality, which is spiritual, manifests only logical sequences to be grasped by the understanding, or relations within a totality. Universalism, on the other hand, accepts the truth of Aristotle's dictum that the whole is anterior to the parts, the idea to its realisation; consequently, it is able to understand groups as wholes, and individuals in terms of the group. The analysis of organic parts (*Gliedhaftigkeit*) takes the place of the principle of causality.

The typical relation, upon which the social order is based, is the relation of friendship, of the master and his disciple (51, pp. 122-30, 89-92). Society is a spiritual phenomenon; one person gives and another benefits, the latter realizing his potentialities, the former being the idea or real essence, which calls the possible into being. Thus the individual receives without submission, and with the certainty that he is realising his potentialities, even while opening his spirit to the gift. Furthermore, individuals are, in themselves, incomplete (*Gezweiung*). They can find the fulfilment which they seek only in and through their relations with others, in friendship, love and the family. These relations are not simple contacts between isolated individuals. The whole is pre-existent; there are friends only because the relation of friendship exists, parents only because the family exists. Individuals are to be conceived (though each retains his moral autonomy and his own being) as parts of a spiritual organism. True, it is possible to seek solitude without being impoverished, but on condition that the solitude is only apparent. The anchorites filled their existence with meditation and God was their companion. The only kind of isolation (*Abgeschiedenheit*) which is fruitful is that of withdrawal from men and community with God (cf. 51, pp. 184-87). Any other kind of solitude means impoverishment.

It may appear at first glance that we have to do, not with a community, but with a multitude of communities; each family, each group of master and disciples, is in fact a community. But these innumerable communities (whose membership is smaller, the more elevated the motives of association) are not simply juxtaposed (51, pp. 238-42). They exist within, and are founded upon, the fundamental communities of language and knowledge. The spiritual objects towards which the various communities are oriented, are interconnected; they are ordered in a hierarchy of values. Thus all the communities are, as it were, contained in the intelligible universe; they are arranged in accordance with a structural law which is both a law of reality and a law of value. This accounts for the hierarchical aspect of society; at the bottom are the masses and the inferior values, at the top are a small number of individuals and the superior values, while below the bottom layer are the negative values of a small number of individuals.

Despite this inherent hierarchy, society needs agencies of socialisation and above all an authentic authority (*Herrschaft*). Here also universalism suggests the basic principle: authority can only rest upon superior value and not upon force and it should be analogous to the validity of truth or the ascendancy of justice. There is no true society where the most worthy do not possess power and enforce obedience and respect upon the inferior. The social hierarchy rests upon a hierarchy of values.

Every social science which is faithful to the doctrine of universalism must start from the study of the whole, and must avoid studying any particular aspect in isolation. Universalism may therefore be treated, as in H. G. Wagner's work, as a variety of sociological theory which replaces the analysis of the economic action of individuals by a study of the economic system as a whole in relation to the social order. But this interpretation, which is valid up to a point, should not be allowed to conceal the other aspect of universalism as a spiritualist doctrine deriving from the romanticism of Adam Müller. It may be added that to assimilate the doctrine to the sociology of Durkheim and Duprat is entirely to distort its meaning.

Sociology is the science of society, of society regarded as the supreme reality, and not, as with Simmel or von Wiese, as a useful concept or a fictitious entity. It is the fundamental social science, and even the special social sciences, though they have a legitimate autonomy, are based upon it. These special sciences are economics (*Volkswirtschaftslehre*), demography (*Bevölkerungslehre*), social statistics, history, *Völkerkunde*, jurisprudence, and the study of morals (51, pp. 510–14)

The subject matter of the science of society proper includes: (1) the fundamental problems of the social order (universalism or individualism); (2) the principles of political organisation; (3) the theoretical bases of all the particular wholes (*Teilganz*), (4) the theory of those particular wholes which are not the object of a special science (science, art, religion, language, the state, law and politics).

I have already outlined the principal ideas relating to the first of these subjects, and propose now to examine the others very briefly.

Justice (51, pp. 151–67) is a principle common to both individualism and universalism, but whereas the former interprets it wrongly as commutative, equalising justice, universalism establishes the principle of distributive justice, which allots to each person his proper station in society and rewards him in accordance with his contribution. Equality is a fundamental truth, if it means no more than the worth of the humanity present in each individual, but not if it means the equal value and equal rights of child and adult, master and disciple, criminal and upright man. In the latter case, equality would lead to atomism and centralisation, and indeed to a Machiavellianism turned upside down, the rule of the least worthy. In reality, there is no equality among men, either in nature or in society. The social bond, which presupposes leader and follower, necessarily implies inequality, just as the totality implies the heterogeneity of the constituent parts. Finally, liberty is the supreme value of individualism, which conceives it as autonomy and the right to personal development, even to licence. Universalism also gives a place to liberty, but only to the liberty of moral self-realisation controlled by objective values, which does not exclude constraint if this is necessary for the harmonious development of the individual or the community. Individualist liberty is only restricted by the needs of security and public order, whereas universalist liberty is limited internally by the spiritual law.

A criticism of this doctrine would lead us too far afield. It is enough to say that it rests wholly upon value-judgments. But Spann refuses to separate science and ethics, sociology and political philosophy. Moreover, his refusal is logical in terms of a doctrine of the nature of society as both idea and norm. The idea precedes the real, the perfect the imperfect, and it follows that the science of society as it exists must concern itself first with the ideal society. The essential structure of society is apparent, though distorted, even in societies which are in decline. Though at times Spann asserts the analytic character of some of his statements (e.g. the basic principles of universalism), he generally mingles the indicative and the imperative. His treatise of sociology is at the same time an exposition of political philosophy.

Spann's account of the structure of society, which could be worked out deductively, is in fact built up from the elements, at first in a formal manner (51, pp. 259–67) and afterwards concretely. If we take as our starting point the human phenomena of *sentiments* (in a broad sense, covering perception, thought, and sentiments in the ordinary sense) and *action*, we have two fundamental processes, the *socialisation of sentiments* and the *socialisation of actions* (the latter being always based upon the former). These processes create the spiritual communities and communal action (*vergemeinschaften* and *Gemeinschaft*, *vergenossenschaften* and

Genossenschaft). Auxiliary processes and structures contribute to this socialisation; first, communication between individuals, which is a prior condition of any community, secondly, organisation which ensures reciprocal action, and thirdly (at a higher level) the political and economic order (the latter defined as the sum of means employed for the attainment of the various social goals). Finally, the community depends upon human dispositions (racially determined) and upon technical abilities.

The material structure, the distinction of the various particular totalities, is more significant than this formal structure (51, pp. 276–84). By "particular totalities" Spann means the various systems in which the whole is expressed and incarnated. Society, like the meaning of a poem or the unity of an organism, does not exist outside its constituent parts. The human form controls all the parts of the body and their relations, but in practice we are only able to apprehend the limbs and organs, and not the whole itself. In society, each objective system of spiritual meaning (such as science) or of action (such as the economic order) is a particular totality. In order to discover these totalities we have only to observe reality, individual and social. Such observation reveals the spiritual systems, science, art, religion, philosophy, morals, and law, and the systems of action (economic order), of co-operative action (classes and estates), of competitive action (politics, war) and of auxiliary action (communication, organisation). Finally, we observe the unitary structures, states and nations, which are the product of the processes of assimilation.

It is not possible, here, to follow the analysis of these various systems in detail. It may simply be noted that Spann's method is strictly conceptual and ideological, without any appeal to observation or experience (except to confirm or illustrate the theoretical propositions). Let us take as an example the sociology of science (51, pp. 285–305). Spann first defines the essence of science (with the inevitable distinction of empiricism and idealism). Science, in so far as it is concerned with truth and falsity, is not social, and is governed by its own laws. The social character of science resides solely in the circumstances of its development, in the fact that society poses the problems of science, or rather that the questions with which men concern themselves in science are linked with the tasks which they set themselves in their everyday life. Society also creates the material conditions for scientific activity and for the transmission of scientific knowledge. Finally, scientific thought is social in the sense that it implies communication, discussion and criticism. The chapters concerned with art, philosophy and religion follow the same plan: first their essence is defined, then their partially social character and the limits of the influence of society upon their development are deduced.

The rest of the book presents a vast body of conceptual thought, which is perhaps useful but does not add appreciably to our knowledge. Even the discussions of theoretical points, though frequently ingenious (for example, the discussion of Kelsen's assimilation of law and the state, cf. 51, pp. 465–67), produce little in the way of results, since the conclusions are derived by deduction from the basic definitions and from the conceptual system as a whole.

What appears most clearly is the outline of a political doctrine which Spann has presented in a more refined and developed form in other books. For example, the concepts of class and estate[1] (*Stand*) (51, pp. 376–85) are opposed to each other in the same way as individualism and universalism. A class is only a collection of individuals with similar destinies, a group considered in isolation and in abstraction from the totality. From the point of view of universalism, on the other hand, an estate is a derivative group, in which common action results from spiritual community; only common spiritual concerns are capable of establishing the estate as a community. In other words, a class, regarded as part of a totality, becomes an estate, and the hierarchy of estates is deducible from the hierarchy of values. Thus the true state is a hierarchy composed of (1) manual workers, (2) higher grade workers (artisans, clerical workers) (3) leaders of industry, (4) heads of the state, (5) spiritual creators and sages.[2]

These observations, though brief, will probably suffice to indicate the tendency of this political doctrine and the character of the underlying philosophy. They will also indicate the various aspects of Spann's work, philosophical (social philosophy, philosophy of history, theory of basic concepts), political, and

---

[1] In the sense of feudal *estates*.
[2] Cf. 51 pp. 384–85. Cf. also *Der Wahre Staat*, Leipzig, 1921.

scientific (a reformulation of economics, as the system of social means, with the aid of the notions of particular totalities and of monogenetic and multigenetic unities). But such distinctions are not really very useful, since there is scarcely less philosophy or political doctrine, and scarcely more science, in Spann's so-called scientific works than in those which are called philosophical.

Conclusion

After so brief a survey it is hardly feasible to draw up a balance sheet, but we may legitimately try to bring out those points on which general agreement has been reached. According to one German sociologist, Geiger, there is agreement:

(a) on recognizing the existence of a special sociology along-side an encyclopaedic sociology, and the distinction between systematic sociology and historical sociology;

(b) on abandoning analogies taken from the natural sciences, and the search for laws;

(c) on accepting, or at least tolerating, a phenomenological method;

(d) on rejecting a pragmatic conception of science;

(e) on giving the concept of society an increasingly abstract and relational character.

The first four items seem to me to sum up very well the characteristics of German sociology, but the fifth would have provoked amusement in the period of the Third Reich.

There is no doubt that the real conflicts of opinion are at the same time philosophical, political and scientific. Consequently, an agreement such as that outlined above does not touch the essential problems concerning method, the sociological point of view, concepts, and the subject-matter and divisions of the discipline. In particular, the relations between general sociology and the various special sociologies are conceived of in different ways. Should economic sociology be limited to the study of interpersonal relations in the economic sphere? Should the development of general sociology make it possible to return to the theory of the different cultural areas and even to the empirical study of groups? Or should economic sociology be concerned with economic activity as part of the social order (as distinct from a separate and analytic study).

Is there any way of summarizing at least the principal results of systematic sociology? According to Vierkandt, it has added to our knowledge the following items: (*a*) the tendency to submission, (*b*) the fundamental social relations, (*c*) the fact that social relations are universally subject to rules, (*d*) the supremacy of communal relations over all others, (*e*) the widening of the individual consciousness beyond the self, and the reality of the collective consciousness, (*f*) the existence of objective social formations of which individuals are only the transient bearers.

But to speak in this context of Galilean discoveries, is only to crush sociology beneath the weight of the comparison and to give a false notion of the significance of sociological activity. Sociology, in fact, does not help us to foresee or to calculate, but only to understand. If we were asked: "What is the use of systematic sociology?" we should perhaps have to answer, "None". But if we were asked "What have you learned from it?" we should be able to reply that we had learned to give up such simple concepts as "constraint" or "imitation", and to understand more fully the infinitely diverse relations between individuals, the conflicting types of social relation, the continual exchanges between individuals, and between the individual and social formations, the existence of individual influences even in the most elaborate social constructions, and conversely the existence of collective influences in the most fugitive individual contacts. Systematic sociology adds to our conceptual resources and refines our sense of reality in the attempt to grasp this life which is at once so intimate and so mysterious.

CHAPTER II

Historical Sociology

In the first chapter I grouped together the representatives of systematic rather than historical sociology; in the present chapter I shall consider those who are historical rather than systematic sociologists. Only Tönnies could be included under both heads. "Community" and "society" are, as we have seen, the two terms of historical evolution as well as two ideal types. Oppenheimer, A. Weber, Mannheim and Scheler, on the other hand, are primarily interested in historical problems. The first attempts to portray the general features of the history of mankind, the second to distinguish the different spheres of the historical world, the third to understand ideas as the expression of historical periods or classes, and the fourth to produce a synthesis of these various attempts. They are all, therefore, concerned with depicting individual instances rather than with grouping the general characteristics of phenomena, with interpreting historical evolution rather than with revealing the nature of society. They concern themselves with objective formations, collective realities (culture, the state, law), rather than with inter-personal relations. Sociology is conceived as being akin to a theory of universal history and as undertaking the tasks of the philosophy of history; namely, the provision of an answer to present anxieties out of the experience of the past.[1]

[1] Thus sociology is distinct from history, as is the study of prophecy from the myth of origins. Cf. Heimann, *Sozialwissenschaft und Wirklichkeit* Tübingen, 1932, p. 25.

I. OPPENHEIMER

Sociology, in Oppenheimer's view, was born with Comte's work, regarded as an attempted synthesis between revolutionary thought and the romantic reaction. Progress and order, liberty and organization, were the two contradictory themes which positivism set out to reconcile once and for all. German sociology began with the attempt of L. von Stein to combine Hegelian philosophy with the social philosophy of Saint-Simon (with a slight admixture of Fourierism).[1] German and French sociology, in spite of their different origins[2] are alike in being attempts to solve the social problem, to overcome the crisis in Western society. This is also the ultimate aim of Oppenheimer's sociological system. He came to sociology from medicine, by way of economics, and he states frankly, even violently, his antipathies and his hopes; in the current terminology, he openly expresses his value judgments. Like the founders of sociology, he could be characterised as attempting a synthesis of capitalism and communism (or a third solution which would bypass both of them). Alternatively his theories might be roughly summed up as a combination of Proudhon's ideals with a historical doctrine derived from Marx and Gumplowicz.

Sociology is very broadly conceived, as being concerned with society as a whole, with historical evolution as a whole, and with the determination of their laws. It is both a special science and the basic science for all the social sciences. It elaborates the concepts essential to all historical research, and reveals the general characteristics of all the various spheres and disciplines of collective life. It differs from encyclopaedic sociology only in refusing to judge the meaning or value of historical phenomena. It conserves the aims, for example, of Comte's sociology. The "dynamic" part is the most important in Oppenheimer's system, and it is preceded, not by a discussion of "statics", but by a theory of groups. Oppenheimer tries to collate the results of all the theoretical and empirical researches relating to collectivities and to the constituent relations of social entities. His work is not limited to a general sociology or to a theory of

[1] Cf. 53, I, 1, p. 41.
[2] This accounts for their different orientations; of the one towards the natural sciences, of the other towards the cultural sciences.

evolution; he adds an economic sociology and intends to complete his work with sociological studies of law and language.

At first sight Oppenheimer's theory seems to be a synthesis, or at least a juxtaposition, of the two tendencies we have distinguished. In fact it is essentially historical, not only because the theory of development and the solution of the crisis which follows from it is the part of his theory to which Oppenheimer attaches most importance, but also because even the theory of groups is impregnated with a historical spirit and with the sense of unique development.

The most general proposition, the basis of political and economic sociology, is that of the falsity of the law of primitive accumulation. Oppenheimer returns unwearyingly in each of his books to this point, which is as decisive in his theory as is the choice between individualism and universalism in Spann's philosophy.[1] In fact, all social theories, whether bourgeois or socialist, accept explicitly or implicitly the idea that inequality and the differentiation of classes are due to an immanent evolution, uninfluenced by any external cause, from a primitive condition of equality or communism. But in reality neither the state nor economic inequality could result from such an internal dialectic. Only force, used by one tribe against another, could account for this historical development.

Oppenheimer refutes this pseudo-law[2] of primitive accumulation from the history of ideas, from theory and from fact. He shows, in lengthy analyses, the origins of this illusion. A purely fictitious state of nature had been considered as real. The golden age of the Stoics, or the war of all against all originally conceived by the Epicureans, were the starting point of a philosophical, and later a juridical theory, and were finally regarded as a reality when the theory became useful to the privileged classes.

In addition, Oppenheimer refutes all those explanations which assume an immanent development. One of the most widespread explanations appeals to the density of population; it is argued that at a certain historical period the scarcity of land made it impossible for some individuals to possess their own land and obliged them to become the employees of those who were more

---

[1] Cf. 53, II, p. 182.   [2] Cf. 53, II, pp. 184–303.

fortunate. But this explanation is open to the following objection: even at the present time, it would be possible, were it not for the existence of large estates, for every man throughout the world and in each country considered separately, to own enough land to subsist on with his family. If therefore it was necessary in the past for some men to become employees, because there was no free land, this must have been because large estates already existed. This monopoly of land ownership cannot be explained in terms of developments within the tribe. An explanation in terms of natural inequalities is also inadequate, since such inequalities are not commensurate with the inequalities of economic condition and social class. Finally, the authority acquired by the stronger or more cunning individuals has nothing in common with the power of the exploiters over the exploited. The strong individual may be the leader or guide in hunting or war, but he cannot become a permanent and arbitrary master; he can direct but not rule.[1]

The facts suggest an alternative hypothesis to that of primitive accumulation which has been shown to be logically untenable. The state results from the conquest of one tribe by another. Its function is to establish this foreign rule and to organise exploitation, and it is the instrument by which the conquerors keep the conquered in slavery, or at least in subjection. By nature it is the outcome of war, and it is riven by internal conflict. Oppenheimer first defines the state as "a territorial group possessing an organisation and equipped with forces for the defence of its frontiers and for the maintenance of law". (ibid, p. 308). He then proposes a more complete definition: "the state is a juridical institution unilaterally imposed upon a conquered people by the conquerors, originally with the sole object of subjecting them to a tribute, as heavy and as lasting as possible, for the benefit of the conquerors". This definition reveals at the same time the *general* characteristics of the state, shown in every historical example, and its *essential* features. Oppenheimer brings forward in support of it a wide range of examples, which show that violence is the origin of every state, and which also reveal the characteristics of the real "state of nature" which precedes political society. His account, though

[1] Cf. 53, II, pp. 232–51.

not evoking an idyllic golden age, is more closely related to this optimistic tradition than to that of the war of all against all. Oppenheimer finds in "natural" groups the sense of reciprocity which is justice. He sees the reign of custom and, on the whole, of peace and tranquillity. There are leaders, of course, where it is necessary to organise a common undertaking, but they are subject to tradition and law, and their authority is based upon age and sanctity; they are neither all-powerful masters, nor despots.[1]

The peoples of the world emerged from this comparatively happy condition as a result of war and of the conquest of agricultural by pastoral tribes, which brought into existence the political state and class divisions. This was the beginning of a long and miserable road by which men arrived at civilisation and approached the final reconciliation.

The long evolution from the establishment of the state to the future Utopia at which Oppenheimer hints, is described in terms of an "ideal type". He distinguishes and illustrates the typical phases in a development which not all peoples have undergone, but which represents, notwithstanding fortuitous variations, a single historical process in the history of the human race. The first stages, those in which there is permanent warfare, the imposition of tribute and mechanical relations, are pre-historical, being the epochs in the formation of the state itself.[2]

In the historical period, two different types of development are discernible, first, that of the maritime state which results in a capitalist system based upon slavery and in rural depopulation, leading to the decline of the ancient world; and secondly, that of the territorial state whose evolution produces the feudal state with its system of estates (*Ständestaat*), absolute monarchy, and finally the modern constitutional state and the capitalist crisis. The historical process is impersonal, or at any rate is one in which the role of the masses is much more important than the actions of great men.[3] Further, this interpretation of history is in terms of the class struggle, for Oppenheimer accepts the Marxist formula: "the history of all hitherto existing society is a

---

[1] *Führerschaft* as opposed to *Herrschaft*, cf. 53, II, pp. 232 and 251.
[2] On these epochs see *ibid*. II, pp. 276–93.   [3] *Ibid*. I, 1, p. 127.

history of class struggle".[1] Finally, this historical evolution, regarded as universal,[2] is presented only in broad outline, and the detail of events is only given, for the most part, in order to illustrate or justify some general statement. The comparative method is constantly used, and even in the case of the modern state Oppenheimer presents a general type rather than historically individual cases. Once again, we can compare this sociological system to Auguste Comte's social dynamics, or to the Marxist interpretation of history, which may be regarded as history, philosophy of history, or sociology according to whether one accepts or rejects the notion of a single process of development, the possibility of discovering its laws, and the legitimacy of reconstituting its typical stages.

The refutation of the law of primitive accumulation served, as we have seen, to provide an explanation of historical origins. It revealed the principle of development (the class struggle). It also serves to disclose the causes of the present crisis, to discover remedies, and to predict the future.

Laisser faire, it is argued, is not in itself a creator of inequality. The contrary belief was long held under the influence of the law of primitive accumulation. In reality, classes existed before capitalism and the two principal features of this regime, the reserve army of labour, and capitalist profit, are the product exclusively of the monopoly of the land, of large landed property. It is this monopoly, in fact, which prevents a normal equilibrium and interchange between industry and agriculture, and which, by provoking excessive emigration from the countryside to the towns, produces the reserve army of labour. As to capitalist profit, it is accounted for, in part, by differences in individual ability, but mainly by the monopoly of land.[3] If there were really free competition there would be a trend towards equality of economic condition, and only those differences due to differences in ability would remain. This being so, it would be enough to end the scandal of large scale property and to institute at last

---

[1] *Ibid.* II, p. 666.

[2] In the fourth volume, where Oppenheimer tries to verify his theory by reference to the facts, the picture becomes more complicated. He adopts some of the ideas of those thinkers who spoke of zones of civilization. Cf. Honigsheim, XI, 1932, pp. 75–88.

[3] 53, II, pp. 680–90.

free competition, for the social problem to be solved and for a society of free and equal individuals to become possible.

Oppenheimer's vision of future society, at the same time a prediction and a utopia, is very similar to that of Proudhon. There are to be no more overpopulated towns, no large centralized states; instead there will be free proprietors, a federal system which is neither centralised nor imperialistic, and a decline in bureaucracy. The ideal is a world society of peaceful peoples, in accordance with the norms of justice as they have been formulated by the Kantian philosopher Nelson, a follower of Fries.

Oppenheimer is the most Western minded (*westorientiert*) of the German sociologists. He is a vigorous critic of racist interpretations of history, and his social ideal is a genuinely liberal society.

This brief summary[1] is not a sufficient basis for discussing Oppenheimer's theories, which are in any case difficult to assess in a short space. The amplitude of his undertaking commands admiration, while his reforming zeal, which sometimes becomes an obsession, calls forth alternately respect and irritation.

II. CULTURAL SOCIOLOGY

A. Weber, like Oppenheimer, is pre-eminently concerned with the present day. Though he advances neither predictions nor utopias, he does not conceal his view that the aim of cultural sociology is to give an answer to the anxious questionings about the contemporary world. We are aware that civilizations decay; are we ourselves on the threshold of disaster or of a new civilization?

Whereas the main concern of Oppenheimer's theory was the social problem (in the nineteenth-century sense), Weber is interested primarily in the problem of culture. He, too, attempts an interpretation of the whole of human history, but in terms of cultural phenomena. He abandons the idea of the *evolution of humanity*, the revolutionary Western tradition, in favour of the notion of a plurality of civilisations each of which has its own individuality and significance, each "equal in the sight of God".

[1] I have been obliged to omit, for reasons of space, any account of Vol. I, which deals with methodology, social psychology, and the theory of groups.

For the somewhat naïve methods of a historiography dealing only with broad outlines, Weber substitutes a conceptual scheme intended to facilitate the understanding of the whole of history. The aim is still to provide a guide to the future and to elucidate human destiny, but cultural sociology is in the first place a scientific theory of history, an attempt to determine the principles of a genuine synthesis, which shall be more than a collection of items, or a series of prefaces.

The first aspect under which historical reality appears is that of spiritual constructions, law, religion and science, within a social framework. Society organizes, directs, and orders human impulses, instincts and wills. The similarities between societies with different cultural systems, express simply the basic uniformity of human nature. The similarities in their inevitable development are explained in the same way; the inevitable succession of youth, maturity, and old age. Nevertheless it is impossible to forecast this development, because one society, according to its relations with others and the influence of its culture, may decay, spread throughout the world, or be destroyed by other societies. Moreover, the inner springs of development do not exclude the influence of other factors, nor of events such as war, accidents, or the emergence of great men. The purpose of this evolutionary framework is only to enable us to understand why events have had an influence at a particular moment; in other words, it is only by the integration of events in the general development that their effects are intelligible.

Among the spiritual constructions which, in the first place, were simply distinguished as a whole from the social framework, we must now in turn distinguish two spheres which are entirely different: civilisation and culture. Positive science and religion are typical examples of these two different spheres. Science is *universally valid*, it has to be accepted by anyone who reflects upon it, and it appeals exclusively to the reason, not to the emotions or the will. Thus it is essentially communicable. Positive knowledge can legitimately be separated from its real foundation. Civilization is a single phenomenon throughout history, and mankind in its advance towards knowledge can be compared, as the well known saying has it, to a single individual who is continually learning.

The disasters which from time to time destroy already acquired knowledge are of little account. They are historical accidents which can neither interrupt the process of civilisation nor conceal its basic unity.

This unity is, if the expression may be allowed, even more critical than real. It is linked with the nature of every rational activity which includes both discovery and mastery. Science is not creation; the world which it reveals existed previously, and we have only illumined, not created it. Natural science and the science of the self alike deal with a real object, which they transform in order to explain. Man constructs a work of civilization which he interposes between himself and nature, but this work arises from reality and is susceptible of application to reality. It is primarily a means of action in the struggle for existence which clarifies the understanding and reinforces the hand.

Civilisation comprises the whole of positive knowledge (of nature or of man), and also the application of this knowledge in techniques. It is at the same time an activity of consciousness (subjective civilisation) and an objective accumulation. These two aspects are not necessarily always in correspondence. The rehabilitation of earlier discoveries by the barbarians is an instance of a consciousness which lags behind its knowledge and at the same time of a subjective civilisation aided by externally acquired knowledge. Thus consciousness develops. It conceives the object and conceives itself with the aid of universal truths (physical science or theory of knowledge, mathematics or moral principles). Civilization leads to the rationalization of human life, and to the transformation of the external world by technology.

Civilization never appears historically in a pure form. Every truth is enveloped in forms originating from religion and myth, and thus their universality is concealed. The various cultures develop unequally the various areas of civilization; nature or spirit, life or matter, are in turn neglected or conceived by men under the influence of their passions and beliefs, or under social pressures. It is not asserted that civilization develops according to an immanent law. On the contrary, the sociologist's task is to show the action of external factors on the development of science and technology. Technical processes, like scientific concepts and theories, are communicable from one culture to another; in spite of interruptions, and temporary setbacks, men are not only agreed in struggling to improve their lives and to extract the maximum output from natural resources but they also appear to make steady progress towards greater knowledge and greater power.

The error of many philosophers of history has been to attribute these characteristics of the progress of civilization, to the historical process as a whole and to fail to distinguish between civilization and culture. Cultural phenomena are to be understood only in contrast with those of civilization. The latter are universal and communicable, whereas the former are *unique* and *incommunicable*, bound to their real foundation, to their living carriers, and incapable of universal validity. In contrast to *a priori*, experimental or practical truths[1] there are the values of modes of expression. In the former case we can speak of discovery, in the latter of invention, or still better, *creation*. In the former we can trace progress, in the latter only sudden productive outbursts, followed by decline, without regularities or law—periods of greatness followed by periods of silence. It is true that appearances may deceive: just as civilization assumes cultural forms, so religion is expressed in propositions and claims to express truth. Faith becomes dogma, and dogma is embodied in a church. Or again, we may mistake a civilizing process in the domain of techniques for an evolution of the arts. Or we may regard the "renaissances", the carrying of religion or art from one society to another, as the equivalent of a transmission of science. In fact, however, a renaissance is almost always a new creation. Primitive Christianity is a unique phenomenon, and the Teutonic Christianity of ten centuries later is another. Classical culture as it appeared in the Renaissance is quite different from the authentic culture of the classical world. In the field of culture there is no genuine diffusion of truth, but only a transfer of unique values.

This contrast corresponds to a metaphysical antinomy. Culture expresses the very soul of a people which the sociologist can neither explain nor analyse, but has to accept simply as a

---

[1] These three types of truths correspond to the three domains of civilization, the theory of knowledge and science of the self, natural science, and technology.

transcendental fact recorded by observation. All cultural phenomena, art, religion, myths, philosophy, are the form of expression, or material embodiment, of a unique soul. Everything else
is material.

The soul can attempt to animate from within, or to give a
spiritual configuration to, the living aggregate constituted by
the social order and the universe of civilization. It is thus that
the periods of synthesis and felicity come into being (Luther,
Mahomet, German idealism), in which the soul finds itself
reflected in the world which it inhabits. At other times, however,
either because it despairs of shaping the intractable material
world, or because it prefers dreams to reality, the beyond to
this world, the soul turns away from the world and loses itself or
takes refuge in a transcendental habitation (primitive Christianity). Or finally, the soul may confine itself to direct self-expression
in products which emanate wholly from itself and in which it
completely incarnates itself (the century of Pericles). Art may
serve as the symbol of desires, dreams, and spiritual activity.

The cultural sphere is less immune than any other from
external influences. In turn, it is able to influence social evolution. It always confronts a constituted whole (*Lebensaggregierung*),
and frequently revolts against a dominant order, whether this
is a purely material world at the beginning of history, or an
order which was at one time consonant with spiritual experience
but is so no longer. Further, the soul is formed in an environment constituted by social institutions and civilization, and
under the influence of, or in reaction to, that environment.
These circumstances are not in themselves sufficient to confer
upon a culture a unique pattern of evolution. In this field there
is neither inevitable maturity, nor ineluctable ageing. The
influence of society is too variable, and the creative activity of
the soul too unpredictable. Consequently, though the sociologist
may attempt to investigate the relations between culture and
society, to compare the external cultural changes in various
historical sequences, and to adumbrate the (possible) laws of
their emergence, he cannot and should not impose an artificial
rationalisation upon an evolution which is the result of spontaneity. It is enough for him to correlate cultural phenomena
and the situations in which they appear, to explain in this way

one of the causes of their appearance and, to some extent, their nature. He does not eliminate or diminish the part played by creative freedom.

Weber's theory is, therefore, pre-eminently a synthesis. Between Hegel and Rickert, between the interpretation of evolution and the logic of science, he introduces empirical propositions, of a very general character, concerning the various spheres of historical reality. Further, he attempts a conciliation between the philosophers of progress (Kant or Hegel) and the theorists of a historical morphology (Spengler), which would result in a real synthesis. The one school sees only an uninterrupted evolution towards an end more or less determined in advance by Providence or by reason, while the other, on the contrary, sees only individual societies which are entirely unassimilable to each other, and which can only be understood, and their development compared, intuitively. The method and conceptual scheme of the philosophers of progress is valid for the sphere of civilisation, while that of the morphological school is valid for the sphere of culture. Both Hegelian and Marxist metaphysics are excluded. Value judgments are no longer regarded as identical with judgments of fact. There is no factor which is at the same time the principle of historical development and a norm of human morality. Further, though ideas are not given the high rank of the Idea in Hegel's philosophy, they are no longer impotent as in Marxism. They are not simply ideologies, or reflections of interests, but on the other hand they are not anterior to the real, nor do they develop in a transcendental sphere. None of these spheres is the cause of historical development, and none is determined solely by an immanent law. The development as a whole can only be understood in terms of the combined action of these three spheres and their reciprocal interaction. Lastly, neither truth nor its cultural expression lose their significance, for there are limits to the determination of ideas by external factors. Thus the aim seems to have been achieved; historical development can be interpreted in the light of cultural development and history as a whole can be understood by an integration, not a mere juxtaposition, of political histories.

At first sight, this theory has undeniable merits. It permits the adaptation of historical method to the real nature of various phenomena. It brings to light the uniqueness of different cultures, without neglecting their interrelations or their common elements, and it maintains the autonomy of the different spheres without obscuring their connection with one another.

It is not possible here to analyse in detail Weber's use of these categories in his *Kulturgeschichte als Kultursoziologie*. I must confine myself to some critical remarks. By what criteria are the various factors to be distinguished? Scheler is inclined to identify the antinomy "being—consciousness" and the antinomy "material impulses—ideal impulses". The material factors are defined by the interested nature of the end (power, wealth), while the ideal factors are defined by the ideal nature of the end. But there is only an artificial correspondence between a theory of human impulses and a theory of historical forces. The historian discloses, in his account of the past, not so much a conflict between egoism and idealism as a double opposition between man and his creations, and between the individual and social groups. He shows the difficulty of finding a place for everyone within social institutions, men's incapacity for organising their discoveries, their rejection of social relations inherited from the past. In such circumstances, all the human impulses influence the behaviour of individuals in all the spheres of society. In the economic field they are not purely egoistic, and in the field of science they are not animated solely by the desire for truth. In every one of their activities the whole personality is involved.

Scheler no doubt was aware of these obvious considerations. And it might be argued that in a particular sphere, for instance the economic, the need for subsistence in all its forms is the primary factor. Nevertheless, it seems to me illegitimate to base a theory of factors upon a theory of human impulses, and to establish a systematic relation between such impulses and a particular sphere of social life. The structure of the historical world is at a different level from that of individual psychology.

The same criticisms cannot be brought against Weber. His distinction between civilization and culture seems to be logical and metaphysical rather than psychological or historical.

Customs, festivals, religious beliefs, are transmitted, or seem to the historian to be transmitted, from one tribe or people to another. Conversely, technical processes are in some cases rejected and remain the property of a single group. But of course, Weber's distinction can still be upheld; it may be argued in the case of the diffusion of a rite or a cult that its meaning is transformed so that the borrower is able to express himself by means of a foreign symbol, or alternatively that it is a case of diffusion within the same culture (which is always possible since the boundaries of a culture or cultural epoch are never rigorously defined). Moreover, Weber recognizes that, in the past, the majority of men were not aware of this distinction between culture and civilization; science was impregnated with religious beliefs, and religious faith was formulated in rational doctrine. It is the historian himself who establishes, within these creations of the mind, a distinction which corresponds to intuited values and not to experienced meaning. Clearly, it is legitimate to interpret dead civilizations in terms of concepts which belong to the present day. Nevertheless, civilization and culture, historically and psychologically integrated in reality, are distinguished mainly by posterior judgment.

Is this analytical distinction at the same time ontological? Weber asserts that it is, but only because he accepts the old metaphysical doctrine of body, soul and mind. If we leave this metaphysic out of consideration, can we regard these three factors as real forces whose combined action determines historical development? It may be asked whether such a conception of development in terms of distinct forces is not the outcome of anthropomorphic thinking, or at least of a somewhat rash simplification. At all events, the list of factors is incomplete; it does not include race or the physical environment. But if these are added it becomes clear that we are dealing with principles of explanation and not with independent forces. Race perhaps determines religion (culture), as the physical environment determines technology (civilization).

To be sure, these categories enable us to sketch the broad outlines of a panorama of human history. But an exact determination of what belongs respectively to culture and to civilization could only be attempted in an arbitrary fashion. The distinctions are useful for obtaining a bird's-eye view of history, but the real value of such a view remains uncertain.

Weber's sociology, like that of Scheler, is the product of a revolt against civilization. Scheler attacks Comte's theory in order to replace the notion of a succession of types of knowledge by the notion of a permanent and essential distinction; philosophy, religion and science, each arising from a different sentiment and reaching different results, are incapable, unless they go outside their proper sphere, of coming into conflict or contradiction with each other. Weber also seeks primarily to demonstrate the autonomy of cultural evolution. The progress of science is in no way a guarantee of spiritual growth. The triumph of civilization marks a return to barbarism.

It is not my intention here to discuss these philosophies or to enquire into the social conditions which gave rise to them. I have only been concerned to indicate the philosophical problems which they raise. In order to construct a universal history which would transcend limited historical chronicles and distinct lines of development, is it not first necessary to analyse the structure of historical reality itself? And if so, does psychology, logic or metaphysics provide the best starting point? Moreover, we may ask to what extent such external explanations are valid, and in particular, what is their significance. It seems desirable, not in order to halt historical research but to determine its limits, to distinguish the various unanalysable phenomena of which the conditions, though not the elements, are ascertainable.

The further analysis of this kind of problem (the explanation of ideas by social reality) will be discussed in the next section.

III. The Sociology of Knowledge

Marxism is a philosophy of universal history. If it is formulated in terms of "factors" or "independent variables" it is difficult to accept in its entirety, except as a justification of practical activity. But for the purpose of the present study we shall distinguish, in Scheler's terms, between a theory of real factors, and a theory of the relation of ideas and reality which asserts the primacy of the economic order and the determination of the ideological superstructure by this order. The sociology of knowledge is a development of this latter problem, or rather of the problems posed by this analysis.

It is, first of all, necessary to be clear about the nature of the problems raised by such an analysis. Marxists dispose of their opponents by the materialist interpretation of ideas, which they claim validates, or at least does not invalidate, their own doctrine. Each class has its own specific style of thought, but only proletarian thought is historically valid. This claim raises the first question; should not the explanation of ideas by the social situation be generalised? How does the historian or the Marxist escape from the vicious circle? How can he justify his own standpoint, and his own judgments?

Furthermore it may be asked to what extent social reality explains ideas. Does it explain their content, or only the moment at which they appear or are diffused? Or is the whole intellectual system, ideas and categories, inseparable from the social situation? Finally, is this explanation also a condemnation? More generally, is the genesis of ideas relevant to their truth value or moral value?

Thus, if ideas which are determined by reality are provisionally described as ideologies, we can summarize the set of problems which Marxism raises in the following three questions: is ideology a general phenomenon? is it universal? and does it imply a value judgment?[1]

These three questions themselves depend upon the philosophy of history or metaphysics which the sociologist adopts. For example, how is the social reality to which ideas are to be related, itself conceived? Is it material or spiritual, a spiritual process of development or an economic process? The choice here will influence the conception of historical evolution and of social classes, and thus that of the relation between ideologies and their bearers, or more generally of the nature of the "determination of ideas by reality". The latter may be conceived as a psychological determination, or as a relation similar to that between a work of art and its creator, as the mechanically determined effect of a relationship of production, or as the expression of an epoch, of a class or of a type of human being.

Such, briefly, are some of the philosophical problems raised

[1] 75, pp. 17–45.

by the sociology of knowledge. The latter may be defined as the historical study of thought connected with reality, that is, of thought whose development is dependent upon social reality and is not purely immanent. The contemporary varieties of Marxism and of the sociology of knowledge, and the numerous theories of ideology all attempt to surmount these difficulties.

The Marxist theories have little in common beyond the assertion, variously supported, that there is a proletarian science (at least a social science) which is incompatible with bourgeois science, and which has a monopoly of truth. Max Adler, the most outstanding of the Austro-Marxists, prefers to the distinction between proletarian and bourgeois economic theory, that between an evolutionary science and a conservative, static science. The distinction is between two theories, two ways of conceiving reality, which employ different categories. One theory is incapable of transcending the horizons of present day society, while the other reveals the inevitable future. If one of them can be designated proletarian and the other bourgeois, this is because there is a psychological affinity between the styles of thought characteristic of the social classes and these two types of science. There is also a relation between the interest of a class and a certain style of thought. Nevertheless, this affinity and the influence of class interest can be overcome; a bourgeois can become a defender of proletarian science, and the truth of a proposition has nothing to do with its genesis, or with the qualities of the person who advances it. Marxism is not a true theory because it is proletarian; its truth can be demonstrated universally, it is valid for everyone, and only from this does it follow that proletarian science is true.

Lukacs, who is a follower of Hegel and not of Kant, attributes a much more profound meaning to the expression "proletarian thought". The historical process is reality itself, and this process becomes conscious of itself in the proletariat which is both the subject and the object of history. Because of its situation only the proletariat is capable of grasping the essence of capitalism, since it directly experiences the naked and inhuman reality of this doomed regime. The bourgeoisie, on the other hand, has a false consciousness, lives in the realm of ideology, separated from reality, and always tends to reify objects, just as our society itself substitutes for human inter-relations, relations between things, or fetishes. The proletariat, like the philosopher in Hegel's system, holds the key to the mystery.[1] He is no longer a victim of the cunning of reason; he knows the future, both theoretically and practically. For proletarian science attains its complete logical adequacy at the moment of revolution, when, by a dialectical transformation, consciousness becomes action. The bourgeois victim of the separation of subject and object and of theory and practice, remains the captive of the things which he has himself created.[2] By contrast, the proletarian never loses his sense of the historical movement as a whole, and he is able to apprehend the truth of the world which he experiences and of the future which he creates.

In their historical research Marxists make use of very varied schemes of interpretation, similar to those of bourgeois sociologists. In fact, they generally agree with Adler in recognising the impossibility of deriving ideas directly from the relations of production. Consequently, some of them, like Lukacs, identify a certain conception of the world, a certain way of life, which are themselves determined by a social situation, in the various psychic productions of a class or epoch. Others simply establish a relation between ideologies and the political and social situation, and the conditions of the class struggle. Others, finally, such as Bogdanov, see a correspondence between techniques and the categories of human understanding, the latter being regarded as reproductions or copies of the forms of work.[3]

Naturally, in the practical class struggle these distinctions become blurred and the theory is simplified; ideologies and even scientific ideas are weapons, and what matters is to use one's own weapons and to turn the edge of those of one's adversary. Hence the desire to denounce the lies, the misrepresentations, the concealments, the convenient illusions and excuses of the property-owning classes. This is a form of historical materialism with which we are very familiar in France. Unfortunately, it is not clear whether it is a question here of the psychology of bourgeois writers (accused of lying or of calculated apologetics),

---

[1] 84, pp. 86 and 165.   [2] 84, pp. 79 and 89.
[3] Cf. the article by Lederer (18, II, pp. 147–71) for an interesting attempt to make the Marxist method more flexible with a view to giving a sociological interpretation of art.

of psychoanalysis, of analysing the structure of bourgeois thought, or simply of a social interpretation of ideas (what is the role of this or that theory in historical development?) Marxists themselves are not always disposed to clear up these ambiguities, from which they profit in controversy.

But although Marxism considered as a sociology of knowledge is perhaps naïvely dogmatic in its outright condemnation of bourgeois ideology and its justification of proletarian ideas, it is not self-contradictory. Marxism does not demolish the notion of truth, but simply decrees in more or less arbitrary fashion that the truth is accessible only to a particular class.

The bourgeois versions of the sociology of knowledge are even more diversified than the proletarian versions; they agree only in refusing the monopoly of truth to a single class. This refusal is perfectly logical in a theory such as that of Scheler. The influence of social factors is only in the selection of ideas, in instigating or impeding their dissemination; it does not determine their content or their value. Ideologies are systems of prejudices, the idols of particular social groups, and though every class is attracted by a particular conception of the world, each individual is capable of divesting himself of class prejudice and of attaining the truth.[1]

It was left to a "bourgeois Marxism", as Mannheim's doctrine has been called, to go beyond Marxism itself and to fall into a thorough-going historical relativism, of which the sociology of knowledge is only the self-styled scientific expression. Mannheim employs the concepts of "total" and "general" ideology; in other words the structure of thought itself, and not merely the content of its results, is "referred to the social context" and considered as an "expression of historical reality"; moreover, no ideas of any groups are excluded from this analysis, all of them being considered as "functions" of reality. Furthermore, this determination of ideas by external factors is no longer irrelevant to their validity. Each group, occupying a definite historical situation, has its own manner of conceiving the world; consequently there are as many perspectives as there are points of view, as many partial truths as there are classes. In an attempt to avoid the naïve dogmatism of Marxism, which asserts that

[1] 86, pp. 203–05.

proletarian ideas are true, while those of the bourgeoisie are false, Mannheim ends by asserting that neither the proletarian nor the bourgeois ideology is either true or false; they are both "perspectives".

This is, in my opinion, the central doctrine of the sociology of knowledge. Mannheim's numerous re-formulations are mainly refinements of it. Let us try to understand how he arrives at this complete relativism (which he terms "relationism" or "perspectivism"). Not all the creations of the mind come within the category of ideology.[1] Mannheim distinguishes various types of intellectual creation, each having its own rhythm of development. In the first place there are the natural sciences and technology (equivalent to Weber's "civilization") which develop by accumulation. The creations of art follow each other without any order, each period and each group finding an original form of expression, a unique style. In this case the essential category is that of *form* and the appropriate historical method is the morphological (Spengler). Finally, between unilinear progress on the one hand, and the succession of styles on the other, there is the dialectical development of custom, law, economics and the social sciences. Here, evolution proceeds from system to system, but all the systems are dialectically bound together; there is repetition but there is also transcendence. The results are taken up on the basis of a new and more general conception, are integrated into a new whole, in such a way as to change their meaning. Thus metaphysics and the social sciences always form part of a whole which expresses a vital experience. The analyses of the sociology of knowledge are concerned with this aspect of organic development.

Mannheim's perspectivism, which is applied to this type of intellectual creation, is derived, not directly from Marxism, but from German historicism pushed to its extreme conclusion. Historicism, in fact, in the post war period, frequently has the two apparently contradictory aspects which are found here: the assertion of the relativity of historical knowledge, and on the other hand, the conservatism of the Hegelian notion that historical development is the development of mind itself conceived as the fundamental metaphysical reality. These two themes are

[1] 71, pp. 37 and 48.

juxtaposed with particular naïveté in Mannheim's early writings.[1] Our knowledge of the past is inseparable from the historian who exists in the present; and our conception of the past will vary according to the point of view adopted, the concepts used and the desires which animate us.[2] Every age and every group re-writes history, but on the other hand all these systems which express historical situations and ways of life complete each other in a total process of development, which we are unable to apprehend but of which we can assert that it has a meaning. The internal dialectic of Mannheim's thought derives precisely from this antinomy between the "perspectivistic" character of all historical knowledge and the meaningful reality of the whole (i.e. the absolute).[3]

The social context to which Mannheim relates ideas is mental, not material; it is a system of human relations, not a physical object. This explains the terms which he uses to refer to the relation between basis and superstructure; it is no longer a question of determination but of "correspondence", of two correlated aspects of a whole rather than an antinomy of authentic reality and its reflection. If we have to begin from the economic system and classes, this is because they are the most solid parts of society, those which are most enduring and powerful, and which have the strongest influence upon individuals who are involved in social relations which they did not will.[4]

Despite these concessions and refinements, and despite his spiritualist philosophy of history, Mannheim nevertheless returns to Marxism. In order to establish his historical theory he criticised Scheler and denied any transcendental meaning to human development, he refused to posit essences, metaphysical or moral truths in an intelligible universe, and he affirmed the fundamental unity of man and spirit, of being and consciousness. It is in and through history that thought and being develop. Thus, since the "bearers" of the successive systems are primarily social classes, one arrives willynilly at a curious kind of Marxism, which is both spiritualist and relativist.

There is no question of a mechanical determination of ideas by facts. Mannheim makes the theory of class more flexible;

---

[1] See, in particular, 71.
[2] 71, p. 37.   [3] 71, pp. 43 and 56.   [4] 72, p. 609.

other groups besides classes can have a unique experience and can express it in a new theory. The relation of ideologies to the social situation may be indirect;[1] an idea may be accepted not for reasons of interest but because it coheres with an ideology which itself directly serves interests or with the way of life of a group. Finally, and most important, it seems to be suggested that it is a type of human being which is expressed in psychic creations, rather than a social reality reflected or projected in a distorted form in ideas.

In other words Mannheim pushes to its conclusion a philosophy of history which affirms that ideas are inseparable from historical development (and thus from social classes). He then attempts to give these metaphysical assertions a positivist appearance with the aid of a social psychology borrowed from Nietzsche or Pareto, and of a theory of man and knowledge, which together establish the unity of being and explain truth in terms of life experience or will.

Once this synthesis (or pretended synthesis) of historicism and Marxism (and authentic Marxism is itself this synthesis of the Hegelian tradition and positivism) has been effected, Mannheim devotes his efforts to three principal matters: empirical studies of the relation between thought and reality; the search for criteria by which to distinguish values, within the sphere of ideologies, without appealing to the notion of truth; and finally, the elaboration of a new theory of knowledge which shall take account of the discoveries of the sociology of knowledge.

It is in the first of these areas that Mannheim's work is most interesting. Here his methods are applied to intellectual constructions of the same type as his own theory, systems of justification and propaganda which are not capable, as wholes, of truth or falsity; namely political ideologies. He reveals the logical structure of political doctrines. Such doctrines are, in fact, syntheses of factual judgments, value judgments, and historical interpretations. The logical structure is not identical in the various doctrines; it depends upon an initial choice which is both voluntary and metaphysical. The involvement in practical activity is derived in each system from a particular philosophy.

[1] 72, pp. 638–52.

Thus liberalism presupposes a universal reason which fixes the ideal to be pursued, while man himself is conceived as being free, like the thinker, to judge reality objectively in order to direct it towards his ideal. At the end of a perhaps indefinite progress actual society will attain the ideal of a society of reasonable beings. The conservative does not believe in this limitless progress, or this human liberty in relation to the real world, or this single ideal. Situated in that part of society which is the product of a long period of development, he conceives historical change as an organic process. Human activity can at most seal or perfect the work of nature; if it is directed towards any higher aim it may lead to chaos. Socialism represents a synthesis; it aims at a future liberation of man (like liberalism), but one which will be achieved by the power of real forces (as the conservative asserts). The inevitability of the future does not make human intervention superfluous, for the choice of the decisive moment is an act of human will. Socialism, the ideology of an oppressed class which sees the future before it, nourishes reformist activity with revolutionary hopes.

The same method as is employed in these sketches of a psychology of political thought, is applied to a more precise analysis of the various stages of conservative thought in the nineteenth century, in what is certainly Mannheim's best work. Without questioning the merits of this study, it may be remarked that it clearly reveals the dangers of the sociology of knowledge. The attribution of a particular way of thinking to a particular social group often appears open to question. For example, the lack of philosophical concern about the bases of scientific objectivity is identified with the indifference of the civil servant who applies rules which he has neither drawn up nor discussed. Whether this is a factual or ideal attribution, it does not conceal the arbitrary character of a method which assumes as its basis a correspondence between ideas and social situation, and which then regards as a confirmation of this dogma constructions which are often only justified in terms of the dogma itself.

In the second domain we have mentioned, Mannheim attempts vainly to resolve the paradox which consists in trying to assess the value of differing ideologies without referring to their truth or falsity. The criteria he proposes are a mixture of pragmatism, historicism, and relativism. They will be mentioned here only in order to show the aims of the sociology of knowledge and its inevitable failure. Certain ideas gradually become the common property of all parties; thus there is a kind of selection which conserves those ideas which are "universally valid". Further, it seems that the most valid system is that which permits the integration of the whole experience of an age,[1] which transcends the preceding system, or which is oriented towards the system of the future. In the same way, if ideology and utopia both transcend reality, the latter will contribute to its own realisation while the former will remain ineffective.[2] Or again, moral judgments which are so incompatible with reality that it is impossible to act in accordance with them, are the sign of a "false consciousness".[3] Finally, ideologies are concepts with which it is impossible to get one's bearings in the world. It is easy to see in all these conceptions the historicist prejudice that one should adapt oneself to the present time and live in one's epoch as if it were unique and allowed only a single attitude towards it. It is easy to see also a pragmatist tendency, which is too vague to have any scientific bearing but which shows an obsession with politics and with the class struggle, expressed in a perpetual suspicion of ideology and in an inability to understand any ideas which cannot be justified by their utility in social thought or action.

It is evident that of these criteria, some are vague while the others assume the truth of that which they are intended to replace. In the absence of an objective history how is the effective utopia, the useless ideology, or even the idea which transcends reality, to be distinguished? The solution which Mannheim seems inclined finally to adopt is that of "perspectivism", with the possibility of a synthesis or interpretation.[4] Every philosophical or social theory is a perspective from which reality is seen, and is limited by the situation of those who are its historical bearers. A synthesis of these partial and biased views can come only from those who, as a result of their own situation, are aloof from parties, relatively independent, and so to speak professionally above the conflicting doctrines. It is the un-

---

[1] 72, p. 636.   [2] 75, pp. 169–80.   [3] 75, pp. 49–55.
[4] See the article "Wissenssoziologie", in *Worterbuch der Soziologie*, pp. 659–80.

attached intellectuals[1] (*freischwebende Intelligenz*) who are to carry out this function, and Mannheim seems to have in mind especially teachers. The fact that in this case the suspicion of ideology gives way to entire confidence, to the hypothesis of complete impartiality (or more precisely of a higher point of view, a total view), may be judged as it deserves. For that matter, Mannheim himself does not seem to be wholly convinced of the legitimacy of this synthesis, and in his later work he appears to abandon it in favour of a possible transfer from one system to another. Just as the physicist takes into account the personal factor, or rather moves from one frame of reference to another, so it should be possible to move from one perspective to another in philosophical, historical and social theories.

But here the absurdity of the undertaking is revealed. It is not possible to "move" from one interpretation of the world to another. The Marxist and the liberal interpretations of an economic fact are not reconcilable. No equivalence can be established between them, since it is a matter of two contradictory interpretations which cannot both be accepted. An empirical judgment is either true or false, in terms of known facts and of logical form. And if a number of rival theories co-exist this must be attributed to the impossibility of verifying them in a strict fashion,[2] not to the existence of several truths or "perspectives" which are equally valid.

Finally, the new epistemology which the sociology of knowledge claims to establish, amounts to no more than ancient and banal ideas, or ambiguities. The criticism of the Platonic conception, which conceives all truths as pre-existing in an intelligible world, and denies the unity of human will and intellect in the conquest of knowledge, is by no means revolutionary. All modern philosophies have dealt exhaustively with these themes. But if the sociology of knowledge claims to dispose of the notion of universal truth itself, to substitute a "dynamic logic" for a "static logic", and to introduce in the form of "relationism" an intermediate form between absolutism and scepticism, then not only does it fall far short of justifying this revolution but it is

---

[1] 75, pp. 121–34.
[2] And also to the fact that value judgments, which are so frequently involved in economic and political theories, are not capable of truth or falsity.

demolished by the ancient argument against scepticism, for "relationism" itself claims to be objectively true.

What, then, is the contribution of the sociology of knowledge? As a theory of knowledge it is nothing, for there is no sociological theory of knowledge. Sociology can only contribute facts or historical interpretations. Durkheim showed that certain simple categories of thought reflect social reality or express the individual's experience of the group. Thus, so far as the sociology of knowledge is identical with a history of categories, it is legitimate. But an explanation of the content of this or that category is not an account of the ability to think in categories, and in any case an explanation of the coercive character of collective representations does not account for the validity of a concept. The theory of knowledge is not history but logic; it analyses the congruence of thought with reality. But collective representations are unconnected with truth; society is the *locus* of inadequate ideas and superstitions as well as of effective techniques and accumulated truths.

Similarly, the sociology of knowledge has contributed no new theory of the relation of subject and object, nor any original analysis of the conditions of truth, nor even an analysis of positive science. It has merely illumined certain aspects[1] of the incontestable and uncontested unity of the scientist and the human being, especially in the domain of social science and metaphysics. Sentiments and desire guide, direct and distort the work of the historian and the economist, and these psychological factors are often an expression of a social situation, that is, of a social class.

In other words, the sociology of knowledge reminds us once again of the difficulties we all experience in thinking impartially in historical, political and social matters. But far from constituting a new theory of knowledge it teaches us nothing about the most important problems of the human sciences, the theory of understanding, historical causality, and methods of verification in fields where an appeal to experience is impossible.[2]

Perhaps I can outline briefly, at this point, some of the diffi-

---

[1] 11, pp. 662–64.

[2] It might be argued that perspectivism is only valid for ideological doctrines, philosophies, historical conceptions, and political theories. But in this case there can be no question of a theory of knowledge.

culties of the problem of ideology, beginning from the Marxist point of view. Ideologies are regarded as being those (false) ideas which serve as the justifications or weapons of a class. Ideology is a refusal to see reality as it is; for instance, the weakness of the mystic who takes refuge in the beyond, the cowardice of the romantic who imagines a fantastic Middle Ages in order to withdraw from the tasks of the present, the dishonesty of the *petit bourgeois* who refuses to recognise his "proletarianisation" and prefers to conceal it from himself by invoking his culture or the superiority of intellectual work, or finally the blindness of the bourgeois who cannot and will not see the fact of class struggle. The polemical vigour of the theory is derived precisely from the confusion of these different cases, a confusion which the metaphysical basis of the theory makes possible (and perhaps legitimate in terms of its own postulates).

The similarity of the different cases can be established fairly easily at the level of psychological analogy. But Marxism goes further, and assumes that there is an authentic, immediate apprehension of the real world, from which ideologies can be distinguished (this is also true of Mannheim's theory). But this apprehension excludes any transcendental metaphysic or religion, the self-styled refutation of which Marx had inherited from Feuerbach. It follows that any transcendental belief fits *logically* (and no longer in a purely psychological sense) into the category of ideology. This is the basis for the criticism of the mystic. Marxism regards the immediate experience of sensuous life and work as real, the supposed interior life being only its reflection, and thus less real than this external activity. From this follows the criticism of the *petit bourgeois*. Finally, Marxism claims to know the essence of present-day society and the secret of the future, and condemns as an error based upon self-interest the refusal to recognise or accept this law of history. This is the basis for the criticism of the romantic and the *bourgeois*.

Is it possible to escape from this confusion of meaning which results from the Marxist theory? In the first place, it must be recognised that the idea of an immediate apprehension of objects, of an authentic reality, is itself an illusion which could only apply to a type of life mechanically adapted to its environment, either by instinct or by omniscience. Man, who is neither animal nor god, and who conceives real objects and values, can only interpret the world in terms of the meaning he attributes to his own existence. The notion of "fleeing from existence" has only a psychological, not a logical, sense. The *petit bourgeois* who refuses to be a proletarian, because he regards culture and sentiments as more important than the amount of his wages, may be cowardly or blind in the view of Marxists, but from the standpoint of logic he merely has a different scale of values. The proletarian who transforms his situation by religious faith, and looks forward to a future life, may be resigned and stupid in the eyes of the unbeliever, but the criticism is just as metaphysical as the belief. Logically, it is a matter of different conceptions of the world. All self-awareness, and consciousness of one's own situation, implies a metaphysic and a moral theory, and what Marx regarded as authentic reality is only the expression of a particular philosophy.

Furthermore, it is clear that "ideology" in the psychological sense implies nothing as to the truth or falsity of the ideas. If a capitalist defends capitalism by arguing that the present crisis is due to external causes of a political nature, his intention may be to justify the economic system with which his interests are bound up, but this intention has no bearing upon the truth of his assertion.

What conclusions can we draw from these two considerations —the illusory character of authentic reality, and the independence of the psychological and logical senses of ideology? Should ideology be defined as a false notion, an error, a limitation, a blindness due to the social position of an individual or class? This is, certainly, a possible definition. But it avoids, rather than solves, the real problem; ideology refers, in fact, to the eternal gulf between history as it is and our knowledge of it, between the historical process as a whole and our limited view of it, but it also transfers the uncertainties of self-consciousness into the social field. Ideology is for a class what self-justification or the resentment arising from an inferiority complex is for an individual. Thus, from the point of view of logic, ideology can only have a psychological significance so long as a metaphysic or a philosophical anthropology has not been able to establish a transcendent truth in the place of the anarchy of desires and preferences. Ideology will continue to have as many meanings as there are doctrines, so long as man is dominated by a historical process of which he believes himself to be the subject but of whose end he is ignorant.

CONCLUSION

The conclusion of this chapter must be as brief as that of the preceding one. Cultural sociology has not resolved the problem of apprehending the whole, and the sociology of knowledge has not resolved the problem of ideology. Oppenheimer did not succeed in establishing the laws of human history. If therefore I had, not to assess the conclusions of this literature (which would only be possible if this essay were concerned with the problems themselves, and not with a group of thinkers), but to indicate its undeniable merits, I should emphasise two essential points. It shows us the themes of the philosophy of history which are widely diffused in contemporary Germany; the plurality of cultures, the ageing of societies, the opposition between culture and civilisation. In France, these ideas either are not widespread or have taken a different form. *The Decline of the West*[1] has had a great success in Germany, but very little in France.[2] Spengler's philosophy in fact runs counter to the traditions of French moralists, with their sense of the individual, of chance, of liberty, of progress and of universalism. It goes without saying that Spengler's demonstration of inevitable decline is far from convincing, but its historical and logical imperfections would not in themselves have interfered with its success in France any more than in Germany, where this kind of prophecy flattered the sense of destiny and the taste for catastrophe, as well as harmonising with the Hegelian tradition of a historical process ruled by laws which transcend the individual. Even those pessimists in France who fear "the death of our civilization" are apprehensive of a (curable) sickness or a (human) folly, rather than of an inescapable fate.

[1] As a matter of fact the book has been rejected by a majority of the official representatives of science. Nevertheless, Scheler, Weber, and Schmalenbach all take up the theme of decadence. Scheler even attempts to give it an empirical justification, in terms of the dominance in each age of a particular striving or category of strivings (desire for power (science) and self-interest in our own age.)

[2] This is less true today. The experience of catastrophe has made the French people more susceptible to historical pessimism.

This literature also gives us a clearer understanding of the philosophy of history implied by all sociology, or more precisely, it helps us to become aware of certain problems which are customarily referred to the philosophy of history but which still dominate every kind of research concerned with the human past; the rhythm of each partial development, the interrelation of these separate processes, the hypothesis of a total process of development, the varieties and uncertainties of the forms of social conditioning of ideas, methods of historical synthesis, the relations of theory and history (or of statics and dynamics), the need to take account of one's own situation in order to understand the exact significance of the discoveries of historical research. In this way we discover the diversity and the subtleties of historical explanations and recognise our own active role in historical research. This is a double progress, in historical understanding and in self-awareness.

CHAPTER III

Max Weber

Max Weber is, without any doubt, the greatest of German sociologists. A jurist, economist, historian and philosopher, he became, finally, the founder of "interpretative" sociology. His work, by its erudition, the variety of questions raised, its rigorous method, and the profundity of the philosophy upon which it is based, has established itself as the paradigm of a sociology which is both historical and systematic.

Much of Max Weber's work is already well known. Every historian knows his *Agrarverhältnisse im Altertum*, and every sociologist knows his *Wirtschaft und Gesellschaft*, the most imposing construction which has yet been attempted in the social sciences. But it is perhaps the case that Weber's personality, and thus the significance of his work, are not so well known. My purpose is, therefore, not to give a summary account of his books (which would be impossible), but to bring out the main features of his philosophy so as to make clear the inspiration and the purpose of his studies.

Weber's originality and greatness consist first of all in the fact that he was, and aimed at being, a politician and a thinker at the same time, or more precisely that he both separated and united politics and science. He separated them, in the sense that science has to be independent of our preferences, and purged of all value judgments. But he also united them, for science is conceived in such a way as to make it indispensable for action. Science is the more useful, the more it is empirical; and politics

67

is the more honest when it recognises that its origins are in desires and when it turns to science for clarification. Weber advocates a science for the politician, and political action based upon science. The historian investigates unique processes of development, and the acts by which men have committed themselves. Politics is the theory and art of irrevocable choices. The synthesis is based upon an awareness of limits which cannot be passed. Neither science nor reality imposes any law; science, incapable of prophecy or of depicting reality as a whole, leaves man his entire liberty. Each individual has to decide for himself.

Beyond the politician, who is the object of the science of the past and an actor in the present, it is man as a whole who appears in Weber's work; man in a divided world where he is obliged to choose between different gods, man in conflict with the destiny against which his faith is shattered. These then are the ultimate themes of the human enterprise which history recounts; competing gods, and the conflict between ideals and necessity.

The Logic of the Social Sciences

Max Weber always declared himself, so far as the logic of science is concerned, a disciple of Rickert. I shall try to show what Weber acquired from Rickert and what he did with it. Rickert's fundamental ideas are well known. The sensible world is infinite and no knowledge can be complete. Science deals with this infinity either, as in the case of physics, by confining its attention to the general and repeatable, or, as in the case of history, by selecting from the phenomena only those which interest us, which are related to human values. Thus a distinction is made between the natural sciences which seek to establish general laws, and the cultural sciences which isolate individual phenomena in order to trace their unique development.

Weber preserves the intention behind this attempt, namely that of establishing the special character and the objectivity of history. One of the strongest prejudices of positivism is to regard as scientific only those disciplines which establish laws. Durkheim's sociology is dominated by the idea that history, dealing with a mass of isolated facts, can never be a science. Weber's sociology, on the contrary, has as its starting point a recognition of history as an objective science of development. This does not mean that, in the field of social phenomena, only the study of unique events or sequences is legitimate or useful. It will be seen later how Weber's sociology gradually becomes distinguished from history. But it is not distinguished as a discipline which establishes laws, or as a genuine science as popularly conceived; it is a complementary discipline, defined by another direction of man's desire for knowledge.

Weber also retains the idea of the infinitude of the sensible world, and of selection by values; but these ideas take on a different aspect in his writings. They are effective weapons against naturalistic prejudices, they contribute to the definition of a method, and they establish within the realm of science the liberty of the individual. Weber's theories always have, in fact, this triple significance, polemical, methodological and philosophical.

Reality is not reducible to a system of laws. The plenitude of the sensible world makes impossible any complete explanation. These observations are equally valid for the reality studied by the natural sciences. Prediction is only successful within closed or simplified systems. We could not calculate in advance the ways in which a shattered stone or an exploding grenade would splinter. This inability does not greatly disturb us, since in this case we are only concerned with the general laws of such events. But in cultural matters, we are interested also in the specific characteristics of qualitative phenomena. No body of laws (economic laws, evolutionary laws) exhausts the task or constitutes the aim of the science of culture.

Weber also regards the "relation to values" as a fundamental procedure in order to apprehend scientifically the singular or unique. In Rickert's work, this procedure is intended to transcend the sensible world, to create a meaningful reality and to establish the objectivity of historical science. It is the case that, in a particular society, all the members accept, not the same value judgments, but the same formal scheme of values. Not everyone considers the problems of the state in the same way, but everyone agrees that these problems raise questions of values, and this is enough to make the selection of the objects of historical science, within a particular group, objectively valid. Moreover, there is at least one value which must be admitted by any science, namely truth. This is sufficient to justify theoretically the idea of a universal system of values, and therefore the possibility of a universal history.

What does Weber make of this notion of selection by values? The first two functions are conserved, namely that of transcending the infinity of the sensible world, and that of distinguishing the field of culture.[1] But it is no longer held that the same objects attract the interest of all historians or of all members of a particular society. It is quite natural that different historians should interest themselves in different aspects, and that they should select their object from the abundance of things in accordance with their particular values. Weber never seems to conceive the objectivity of history as founded upon a universal system of values. On the contrary, such a system (supposing it to be possible, which Weber questions) would be a matter for philosophy and not for science. Further, while Rickert emphasised the need to relate facts to the values of the period studied, Weber refers principally to their relation to *our* values. The past is brought into relation with the present. Or rather, *we* ask questions of the past, and without such questions there would be no historical science.

It follows, that *there is no objective science of the entire past or of society as a whole.* Any science of culture is partial (even if it establishes laws) because its point of departure is *legitimately arbitrary.* It can only be a positive science if it is conscious of this unavoidable limitation. It establishes objectively the causal relations which explain the development of one sector of reality. Consequently, it leaves intact the freedom of the politician, while showing him the means by which to attain his end (in this way the scientist chooses his object). The relations are still closer; the choice of the historical object is determined by the value strivings of the politician. Finally the methodological theme becomes a philosophical conception; the historical flux moves towards an unknown end, always presenting new meanings and new spiritual constructions. In the face of a world which is always new, man does not and will not cease from renewing his curiosity and his knowledge so long as "an ossification of our minds, in the Chinese style, has not made us

[1] Or rather, that of isolating within the cultural field the object which interests us.

unaccustomed to posing continually new questions to the inexhaustible wealth of life".

I have shown briefly the place which Rickert's ideas occupy in Weber's thought, in order to emphasise the unity of the man and his work. But it is clear that his methodological principle does not lose any of its rigour for being infused with philosophical intentions. The choice of an object means an enlargement, not a narrowing, of the historical vision. Durkheim invokes *the* unique and definitive sociology of the future which is to supply *the* system of social laws, and believes that he already possesses *the* classification of societies. Weber opposes to this dogmatism the legitimate multiplicity of approaches and researches, corresponding to the diversity of the spiritual worlds which human societies create. It is the whole man who is the central concern of history and sociology, and the historian who asks questions of the past has the right to become completely involved in the questions which he poses.

But this liberty is not anarchy, for once the choice has been made the historian must submit entirely to reality. Once the historical object is determined, we are no longer free either in the choice of material (which is fixed by the values involved) or in the establishment of causal connections. In other words, the relation to values is a means of subjecting a cultural reality, made up of human desires, to objective study.

The special character of the cultural sciences results, in Rickert's system, mainly from the uniqueness of historical phenomena and from the selection by values. These ideas form only the introduction to Max Weber's work, the two essential aspects of which are a theory of scientific concepts, and a definition of historical knowledge as a synthesis of *understanding* and *causality*.

The "ideal type" should be regarded less as a distinct variety of concept than as a generic name for all the concepts used by the cultural sciences. The ideal type is related to two other features in Weber's thought: first, a thoroughgoing nominalism, and secondly, a conviction that the concepts applied to cultural phenomena cannot be reduced to the framework of traditional logic.

Idea and reality, the general and the particular, "ought" and "is", are always distinct. What "is" cannot be deduced from any law. Concepts are simply indispensable instruments for apprehending the world, and they are always being transcended by a knowledge which only progresses by transcending them. Thus it is necessary to define rigorously the terms employed, not in order to turn science into a closed system, but in order to compare our ideas with reality and then, having realised their inadequacy, to attempt to make our thinking more profound. The function of the ideal type is to make such comparison possible and fruitful.

Furthermore, Weber opposed the ideal type to the concepts of traditional logic and to average types. How could capitalism, liberalism, socialism, or the State, be defined by the rule of *per genus proximum et differentiam*? It is equally impossible to define the "romantic" or the "Greek" or the "entrepreneur" in terms of characteristics common to all romantics, Greeks, or entrepreneurs, or even in terms of an average of the qualities of individuals belonging to these groups. In practice, we carry out a "stylisation", and retain only what seems characteristic; we construct a type. Thus the ideal type is defined as a mental construct obtained not by a generalisation of the features common to every individual but by a Utopian rationalization. We bring together characteristics which are more or less evident in different instances, we emphasize, eliminate, exaggerate, and finally substitute a coherent, rational whole for the confusion and incoherence of reality.

It is obvious that these two features are not sufficient to define the ideal type. But it would be difficult to advance any further along this path, since here, as in all the problems of logic and philosophy, Weber is an *oppositional* thinker. He only suggests indirectly the more detailed characteristics and the varieties of the ideal type, in his critical discussions of the scientific and metaphysical theories which he rejects or refutes.

The ideal type is, in the first place, a concept which is opposed to the *concepts of essence*, and represents, so to speak, a positive substitute for them. There are no essences except in relation to, and by means of, a value judgment. "Authentic Christianity" or "true socialism" are the product of the preferences of the historian or the theologian. Such notions have no place in positive science.

Weber, in harmony with the Kantian tradition, renounces all but empirical knowledge; modern science does not go beyond the ordering of experience and the establishment of causal relations. We have abandoned the illusion that knowledge can attain to the essence of things, the true being behind appearance, the laws of God and of Nature. In the same way, in the field of culture, essences such as *Volksgeist* (the spirit of a people), and holistic concepts applied to phenomena such as the State or the Church, to which we are inclined to attribute a unity and a transcendental existence, have to be abandoned. They go beyond the scope of scientific knowledge and obstruct attempts at explanation. Once these metaphysical substances have been rejected, man becomes a free agent in the world of immanent experience. Similarly, science, freed from essentialist prejudices, is able to construct, out of any historical phenomenon, a multiplicity of ideal concepts, according to the direction of our interest and the needs of research. We are doubtless ignorant of the spirit of capitalism. But we can freely create ideal types of capitalism: e.g. an economic system motivated by the pursuit of private profit, or a rationalized economic system in which enterprises, separated from the family and organised in accordance with definite rules, produce for the market and use free labour. There are no true or false definitions, but only definitions which are more or less fruitful.

The ideal types emancipate us from naturalistic prejudices as well as from metaphysical illusions. The positivist is tempted to regard as essential those characteristics which are universal; he would define religion *essentially* by those characteristics which are present in all religions. He then strives to establish *the* valid definition; at the beginning of his enquiry he chooses the characteristic which is most obvious or most frequent, and hopes to arrive in due course at a complete definition (assuming that he does not, by degrees, come to regard his initial definition as adequate). On the contrary, in Weber's work, still more than in his theory, the ideal type is employed to discover the *unique features* of each historical phenomenon. His definition of capitalism is obtained by distinguishing those facts peculiar to Western civilisation, or at least especially developed in this civilisation. In its application to historical entities the ideal type, as distinct from the general concept in traditional logic and in positivism, is intended to reveal individual and unique characteristics rather than similarities or general features. The ideal type can be used equally well in formulating a problem (how did capitalism, regarded as the achievement of a particular kind of organization of labour which is only found in the West, originate?), or in expounding the results, or in research (to what extent does reality conform to the ideal type?).

The ideal type, which expresses the scientist's liberty to determine the object of his enquiry and which is an instrument of a science of the particular, becomes clearer by this twofold contrast with essence and universality. It is further defined by the elimination of any confusion between itself and reality. Such confusion is particularly easy since ideas and ideals are also real phenomena (of a psychological order). If, for example, we construct an ideal type of liberalism, we are concerned with liberalism as a political system or as a human attitude. But liberals themselves had a certain conception and a certain ideal of liberalism. We can, therefore, also construct an ideal type of the liberal ideal. It is important to be always aware of this distinction between the ideal conceptions held by individuals in past ages, and the ideal types of which we are speaking. A particular legal rule has an influence upon conduct through the conceptions which it produces in the consciousness of individuals. The philosophy of law and jurisprudence also have an effect through the conceptions which they produce. It may appear, therefore, that in this case we can identify the ideal meaning of a law, or of a body of legislation, with reality. But Weber insisted upon a careful distinction between law as a norm and law as fact. For the sociologist, a law signifies only a certain degree of probability that specific actions will be followed by other actions on the part of other persons. The ideal type of a law, or of a body of laws, and the constructs of science or of jurisprudence, are used as instruments for research, for circumscribing the object of enquiry, and for formulating a problem.[1]

[1] This does not, of course, prevent Weber from studying, as well, the meaning or meanings of legal rules.

In other words, the ideal type can be deduced from ideal or normative realities without changing its character. It is only necessary to distinguish between the sense which *we* give to a rule in our ideal construct and the sense which it had for the men who conformed to it or the jurists who interpreted it. Sociology is concerned with the experienced meaning.

Finally, the ideal type is defined (and this no doubt is the essential point) by contrast with a too ambitious interpretation of economic theory. The so-called classical laws are only a body of ideal-typical constructs; they are instruments of knowledge and not final results. The marginal utility theory, for instance, is not based upon psychology. It indicates what would happen if the behaviour of individuals were similar to the decisions of a merchant continually engaged in the calculation of his liabilities, assets and requirements. It has to be verified empirically; or at least we should try to determine the gap between this ideal type and reality.

The theory of ideal types is, no doubt, incomplete. Perhaps we should distinguish between historical types (modern capitalism), general types (bureaucratic power), and types of rational behaviour (economic theory). Nevertheless, in this case as in others, Weber has grasped what is essential. What needs to be done, in addition to making the distinctions we have just mentioned, is to examine more closely and to make more precise the idea of methodological rationalisation, so as to give full significance to the twofold requirement of causal adequacy and adequacy of meaning.

The uniqueness of the cultural sciences is above all due to the particular satisfaction which human curiosity obtains in this field as a result of "understanding".[1] In the domain of culture positive science apprehends a meaning which, in the study of nature, is only accessible to metaphysics. It is difficult to define "understanding" strictly and Weber himself does not so much define it as suggest its characteristics. He refers to the special kind of evidence associated with the apprehension of meaningful relations, such as those between motive and act, or between end and means. We have an impression of being able to repro-

[1] Cf. 101, pp. 67 sq., 93 sq., 403–17, and 503 sq.

duce in ourselves the process of consciousness which we identify in other people.

This transcendence of sense data was, in Weber's view, a characteristic of the cultural sciences, since it allows us to explain an event in its uniqueness, rather than in terms of a general law. Moreover, it leads us beyond a simple ordering of experience such as that of the natural sciences, and provides a means of taking into account the specifically human character of the phenomena we are studying. In other words, we can say that interpretative sociology, in contrast with Durkheim's philosophy, treats the historical world not as a collection of objects, but as a process of development of human lives.[1]

Weber's theory of understanding is extremely difficult to study because its basis is ambiguous, and because, once again, it is used only in controversy. The concept of meaning, which is associated with that of understanding, is likewise obscure; does meaning, as with Rickert, occupy a third sphere between the physical and the mental, or does it denote an aspect of mental phenomena? On the whole, Weber is inclined to accept the latter view, probably under the influence of Jaspers. Further, Weber criticises at length those theories which distinguish the sciences in terms of the objects studied rather than in terms of the directions of human curiosity. The peculiar features of cultural phenomena have an influence upon method, since they permit the supplement of "understanding", but they do not impose the basic principles of individualisation and reference to values. Above all, Weber denies that intuition has a different role in the cultural sciences from that which it has in the natural sciences. The cultural sciences arrive at valid judgments and make use of rigorously defined concepts. The starting point of history is lived experience, but in order to establish a science, this confused experience has to be analysed with reference to values.

Further, relationships, no matter how obvious, are never anything more than hypotheses as long as the motivation to which they point has not been analysed. In other words, Weber wished to establish two principles: first, that there is no immediate

[1] J. Monnerot has taken up this theme in his book, *Les faits sociaux ne sont pas des choses*.

apprehension of the object in the cultural sciences, and secondly that science requires an analysis of the given fact and a series of researches in order to establish causal connections.

In order to make more precise the notion of "understanding" it is necessary to refer to Jaspers' conception from which it is derived. Jaspers opposes interpretative relations and causal relations. Understanding is an ultimate datum; the person who has been deceived takes his revenge, the angry man wants to attack his adversary, and so forth. We understand such relations directly; no science can make them clearer to us than they were at first. A causal relation, on the contrary, such as that between the destruction of cortical tissue and aphasia, cannot be understood; the regularity of succession allows us to formulate a rule which we then try to subsume under a more general law. For the psychologist, therefore, there is an absolute distinction between an interpretative relation and a causal relation. The interpretation of behaviour in terms of resentment is incommensurable with its explanation in terms of a condition of the nervous system. Weber's central notion is perhaps best apprehended if one thinks of the need to establish a connection between understanding and determinism. The psychologist is satisfied with the intelligible relation between resentment and a certain type of behaviour, but the sociologist and the historian wish to account for a particular action in terms of resentment. How in fact, is it possible to validate an interpretation which, however obvious it appears, remains a hypothesis in the particular instance being considered?

The rational character of the conceptual schemes employed further reinforces, if it may be so expressed, the hypothetical character of the relation. A rationalising method does not imply any particular conception of human psychology, and still less a metaphysic. No doubt we are tempted to explain human beings in too rational a way because this type of explanation is the nearest to hand and the most convenient, but in every case it is necessary to find out whether our interpretation corresponds to the facts.

Every intelligible relation is by nature hypothetical; this is a fundamental ambiguity. Different individuals react differently to the same external situation. The motives which the individual attributes to himself may be pretexts or justifications; within the consciousness of each individual there is again an ambiguity. Finally, in an identical situation, individuals are struggling with contradictory desires. The interpretative relation is possible as long as it has been demonstrated to be a causal connection. In the case of a particular action we have recourse to explanations which are more or less verifiable (which take account of the knowledge we possess of the person concerned). If it is a question of formulating a rule, repetition (and occasionally statistics) allow us to transform the possible into the actual.

Psychology can contribute to understanding but has no decisive rule. Following Rickert, Weber refused to regard psychology as the basic discipline of the cultural sciences. So-called scientific psychology seemed to him of little value to the historian, since it had a different aim, namely the establishment of laws. The general propositions to which the historian has recourse are, in Weber's view, those of the "wisdom of nations" or of common sense, which it would be pedantic to formulate. The sociologist can and should make use of a more refined psychology, an interpretative psychology such as that of Nietzsche or Freud. Such a psychology does not, however, enable us to choose between the various interpretations which it suggests. For this, whether we are concerned with a single action, or with a type of action, it remains necessary to show that one of the possible relations is the real one, and this is a task for the historian or the sociologist since it requires the introduction of causal explanations. Moreover, it is almost always necessary for us to understand the reaction of an individual to a particular situation, and no psychological factor can account for this. What we have to grasp is, above all, the intention, the combination of means in order to attain an end which is suggested or imposed by the circumstances.

Thus we are always led back to the central problem of single causal connections. In order to be valid, the science of development, of which the point of departure is subjective, must attempt to establish objective relationships. The ideal types are only constructs which are useful in understanding or explaining phenomena, while the interpretative relation is valid only so far as it is also causal. What theory meets these requirements?

To seek the causes of an event is not to reduce succession to a law; this procedure of the natural sciences would eliminate history. The latter attains its end by integrating the particular event which we wish to explain in a unique complex of events. For this, it is indispensable to make a selection among the consequences and to limit the antecedents which are taken into account. The primary condition for establishing historical causality is this selection. It is impossible to give an account of the whole of reality, and a historical cause can only be defined with reference to particular aspects of a given phenomenon. Thus, if one studies the origins of capitalism it is essential to state those aspects of capitalism which are to be taken into consideration. A causal relation cannot be established between one total situation and another, or between one historical moment and another; it is never more than one strand in the whole, and is only established by a conceptual transformation of the crude reality.

The selection of antecedents is carried out in the following way: In order to determine the importance to be attached to a particular antecedent we have to conceive it as changed or non-existent. We then attempt to visualise, on the basis of our general knowledge, what would have happened in these hypothetical circumstances. If the phenomenon whose cause we are studying would have been different in these circumstances, in respects which come within our field of interest, we can attribute these aspects of the phenomenon to this particular antecedent (without implying that it was the *only* cause). This approach, which may appear difficult in the abstract, expresses a very simple idea. If we are studying the causal significance of the battle of Marathon we shall ask ourselves: What would have happened if the Greeks had not been victorious?—and we shall try, not to imagine the detail of events (for this would be an impossible task), but to determine whether the evolution of Greece would have been different in one important aspect or another. The battle of Marathon will then be regarded as *one* cause of these aspects. Can we, in fact, reconstruct the evolution which the victory of the Greeks prevented? Such a reconstruction is possible, since a study of analogous cases, such as the conduct of the Persians in those countries which they conquered, enables us to visualize the theocratic regime which might have been established. The difference between this hypothetical evolution of Greece under Persian rule and the evolution of Greece as an independent nation, indicates the importance of this battle which, from a material point of view, was insignificant.

This conceptual scheme, which in Weber's view only made explicit the practice of all historians, can be applied equally well to a limited event as to large scale phenomena. Using Weber's own examples, it is just as essential for analysing the motives which have led a mother to slap her child, as for determining the causes of capitalism. For to say that if the mother had not been exasperated by her cook she would not have slapped the child, is to suppose an antecedent eliminated and to infer that the event would then have been different.

It will be objected, no doubt, that this scheme is useless as long as we do not have the knowledge which would allow us to reconstruct in a valid manner the hypothetical evolution. But we have no need to describe in detail what would have happened; it is enough for us to know that things would have been different. Further, the comparative method is intended to facilitate these hypothetical reconstructions. And finally, we are not seeking necessary relations, but trying to establish adequate or possible relations.

The evolution of Greece under Persian rule, as we imagine it, cannot be described as necessary. Without even taking into account the subjective probabilities, associated with the imperfections of our knowledge, the facts which appear to us to determine certain consequences create in reality only an objective possibility. Fortuitous events would have been added to these basic conditions and might have changed the course of development. Consequently we can only say that a development towards theocracy would have been an adequate effect of a Persian victory, in the sense that the circumstances would have produced this result in the majority of cases. Similarly, if we assert that a revolution was inevitable in 1848, we simply mean that the basic circumstances, combined with a large number of antecedents, would have produced this revolution (or rather, would have combined with a number of antecedents which is very large in comparison with the number of those which would not have produced the revolution). In the same sense, one might say that a circumstance renders a certain effect more likely if it increases the number of favourable accidents. On the contrary, if it is held that the firing on the boulevards was the real and fortuitous cause of the revolution, this implies that the revolution is not adequately explained as the result of a particular set of antecedents (the number of accidents which, added to these antecedents, would have produced the revolution was small). It is admitted that it was fortuitous in relation to these antecedents. Thus the two notions of adequate and accidental causality, of law and accident, are reciprocal, both being based upon arguments of probability.

This theory of historical causality poses a number of problems. How are the antecedents to be selected? Does not the determination of rules and of accidents involve circular reasoning? Further, though an event is an accident in relation to one group of antecedents, is it not at the same time a necessary effect in relation to another group, so that these two notions are, as it were, completely relative? Do we possess experiential rules which confer a sufficient degree of probability upon our reconstructions? At what level, and at what stage, can we and should we raise the question of probability?

Despite its incompleteness this causal theory proved adequate for Weber's work. As we shall see, it forms the framework of his studies of the origins of capitalism. One of its chief features is that it entails a continuous collaboration between history and sociology. Causal imputation requires, in fact, the establishment of rules, not in the form of laws, but of frequent succession between two types of event (the influence of specific circumstances upon other specific circumstances); certain conditions facilitate, or in the most favourable case have as adequate effects, a certain type of behaviour, or again, certain economic phenomena are associated with certain legal institutions or religious attitudes. We have before us, therefore, a history which does not ignore irregularities and a sociology which does not eliminate either accidents, or ideas, or human strivings. The historical world as a whole, with its dramatic character, can find a place within these categories.

By means of this causal reasoning we are able to transport

ourselves to a vanished actuality, and to give life to potentialities which were never realised, in order to become aware of the events which determined what appears to us as destiny. By an appropriate selection of antecedents we can distinguish human decisions from the external circumstances and thus discover those acts by which man has made his history.

This conception of causality seemed to Weber not only reconcilable with an interpretative explanation in terms of motives, but also indispensable to the objectivity of science. In his view, only causality assures the universal validity of a scientific proposition, and he came to regard all the non-causal forms of understanding as nothing more than an introduction to research. The understanding of a work of art, of a spiritual creation, or of a human mind, was, in his view, only an analysis of values. Genuine science is causal explanation.

POLITICAL THEORY AND POLITICAL ACTION

There are two ways of interpreting Weber's theory, both of them legitimate; one is concerned with its scientific aims, the other with its philosophical aspirations. On the one hand there is the intention of establishing the objectivity and uniqueness of the cultural sciences, and on the other, that of making a logical distinction between science and politics, so that they can contribute, by their very separation, to the unity of the human person. We have already outlined the methodological themes, and can now go on to discuss the philosophical conceptions in their three main aspects: the logical distinction, the contribution of science to politics, and the stylistic analogies between the work of the scholar and the politician.

The logical distinction is based upon a radical separation of fact and value, of factual judgments and value judgments, of science and morality. The historian, the sociologist, and the economist, can and should abstain from taking sides, from praising or condemning, for pure science is incapable of resolving the problems of action. It may be objected that this exclusion of value judgments is banal, that it is proposed by all sociologists, and that at the present time it is not very useful. It would be easy to reply by pointing to the contradiction between the practice of sociologists and their theoretical principles, but in fact, the confusion of these two spheres, or at least the hope of reuniting them and the belief that such a reduction of one to the other is possible, still persists in the realm of theory itself. Auguste Comte's dictum that there is no liberty of judgment in astronomy or physics, and that there will be none in politics once sociology has been perfected, is the implicit or explicit credo of most French positivists. All such attempts as the deduction of a practical art from a science of morals, the establishment of a new morality on the basis of sociology, the elevation of the moral consciousness and of moral commands to the level of universal truth, result from the same illusion or the same belief: that there is a scientific solution of the ultimate problems of conduct.

It was this theoretical confusion rather than the practical one which Weber criticised, since it seemed to him to reveal a misunderstanding both of the nature of modern science and of the conditions of ultimate choice. It was not only dangerous for scientific truth and moral honesty, but it also endangered the dignity of the human person.

The impossibility of scientific value judgments is due at the same time to the limitations of science and to the nature of moral decisions. Science, as we know, is incomplete; it establishes objectively valid relations of causality, but it does not embrace reality as a whole, does not reduce it to a system of laws and does not predict its inevitable future. It can, no doubt, indicate the means necessary for the attainment of a given end, by a simple reversal of the relation of cause and effect. Moreover, science is essential in order to decide upon the means, and to estimate the price which we have to pay for a particular result, for we have to take account of the secondary results, undesired but inevitable, of our acts. Finally, interpretative science enables us to become aware of our own strivings. By the interpretation of values, by the confrontation of diverse doctrines, we are able to discover the reasons for our self-contradictions, and consequently to deduce logically from the supreme values the attitude to adopt in a particular case. Science reveals to us what we *desire* and what we *can* attain, but not that which we ought to strive for; it leads us to self-knowledge and to knowledge of the world. Beyond that is the sphere of desire and will.

Even if science should prove a particular aim to be impossible of attainment, even if it should show that circumstances make our revolt futile, man is still not deprived of his autonomy, for he is not obliged to seek success.

The ultimate antinomy which each of us has to resolve, is that of the inescapable choice between a morality of inspiration and a morality of responsibility (*Gesinnungsethik* and *Verantwortungsethik*). Either we swear to obey the law, whatever may happen, or we try our best to change the world in the direction we desire, to foresee the consequences of our acts in order to triumph over determinism and avoid bringing about, in the last resort, a situation contrary to that at which we aimed. Does the value of our acts derive from our intentions alone or from the consequences of these acts? Do we accept the excuse of the politician: "I did not intend that"? Do we accept the justification of the Inquisition: "It is for the good of the church"?

Weber liked to quote two examples of a purely inspirationalist morality; the sermon on the mount and the attitude of the revolutionary syndicalists. As to the morality of responsibility, he saw its caricature in the *Realpolitik* of many of his contemporaries, and a genuine example of it in the Florentine who sacrificed his own personal salvation to the salvation of his city.

Though the choice of a (purely formal) maxim determines our whole attitude, it is nevertheless not the only choice which is forced upon us. The heterogeneity of ethics and of cultural values, the irreducible and irreconcilable plurality of cultural values, make our whole existence "a series of ultimate choices by which the soul chooses its destiny". The multiplicity of gods expresses an ineluctable struggle. No doubt it is possible to conceive of a religious metaphysic which would establish a definitive hierarchy of values. But for science, and for an existence which does not recognise a beyond, this rivalry of gods is a basic datum. We know that an object may be holy *because*, and not *although*, it is ugly, or that it may be beautiful *because* it is immoral. Existence consists in choosing between different gods.

In political life, especially, we have to choose a definition of the values which everyone claims to respect. Does justice mean the compensation of natural inequalities, or on the contrary, the reward of the best and the most highly gifted in accordance with their merits? Further, does the end justify the means? Must the individual accept moral delinquencies in order to be useful to the supra-individual reality which he serves?

The rejection of scientific value judgments is thus connected with Max Weber's deepest personal strivings. It is not a simple methodological precept but a kind of scientific asceticism which expresses a desire for purity; its aim is to exclude the passions from scientific research, in which the individual tries to be entirely rational in order to acquire exact knowledge, and to confine them to the sphere of action, in which man is responsible but free from all constraints and in which he engages his whole personality.

It is difficult to grasp the magnitude of Weber's political activity. He was never really engaged in political action, and he had no political doctrine in the ordinary sense of the word. We cannot here investigate whether this failure in practical achievement is to be attributed to external circumstances, to his illness, or to his character. As to the absence of a political doctrine, it is necessary to examine its significance. Weber's political thought did not involve a system. He did not have any abstract knowledge of the "best form of government", and he believed neither in popular sovereignty nor in sovereignty derived from God or tradition. There is no politics except in the world, and no action except in the present.

Though Weber's work is not a system it is still less a collection of "opinions". He did not have any more or less vague tendencies in this or that direction. He did not desire a less rationalistic and more emotional civilisation, and he did not dream of eliminating real conflicts by a spiritual revolution. His politics were not those of a *litterateur* or moralist, but those of a historian and man of action. They were not a system, or a collection of mere opinions, but judgments. To act is to make a decision, to deal with events, and to aim at an end, in a unique situation which one has not willed. Political philosophy, therefore, can be nothing but a more profound understanding of temporal action, a reflection upon the conditions within which our desires are expressed and an analysis of political choices in their relation both to reality and to our ideal.

Weber, faithful to his theory, exemplified throughout his life this kind of reflection, applied to historical development, in order to grasp the moments when human will is able to intervene effectively. On every occasion he judged what, in terms of the facts and of *his* values, should be attempted. He has left a record in his articles and books of the kind of action which he would have liked to accomplish. He was prepared at any moment to answer the question which disconcerts all our amateur politicians: "What would you do if you were a Cabinet minister?"

Thus it is possible, without undue artificiality, to distinguish in his political writings: (1) a theoretical part which analyses (*a*) the permanent, (*b*) the present, and (*c*) the personal, conditions of political action, and (2) a practical part containing assessments of particular situations and historical judgments.

The theory[1] is dominated by the antinomies: morality of inspiration and morality of responsibility; means and ends; morals and politics. Indeed, these antinomies appear with particular intensity. It is only too evident that evil may result from good; for example, to disarm in accordance with the pacifism of the Gospel is to expose oneself and to allow one's enemy to impose a victorious peace. Yet only a righteous peace would really discredit war itself, whose absurdity would then become apparent to all. The Communist who gladly accepts a continuation of war for two years, if the revolution will be its outcome, declares that in this case at least the end justifies the means. Every politician has to resolve this antinomy for himself and to decide when the end does justify the means. We are never able, in striving to attain our ends, to use only such means as conform to our ideals. Every politician is in some degree Machiavellian.

In this there is something more than an occasional discrepancy resulting from the irrationality of the world or the folly of mankind. The State is the institution which disposes of a monopoly of legitimate violence, and politics is essentially a striving towards power, or at least an attempt to redistribute it. The true politician does not seek power for its own sake, or with the sole purpose of enjoying its exercise. He has in view a further aim, the greatness of a collectivity, the diffusion of a culture,

[1] Cf. "Politik als Beruf" in 106, pp. 396–550.

justice in social relations. But the necessary means is power, with violence in the background. The early Christians knew well that whoever engages in politics "makes a pact with diabolical forces", for the world is "ruled by demons".

Weber does not make much of the traditional distinction between private and public morality. He sees in this only a special case of those conflicts between autonomous spheres of morality which every individual has to resolve. The moral rules vary significantly in the different spheres of the individual's activity, in the family, in public life, in his occupation, and in the relations of friendship or love. True morality, that of the sermon on the mount, or that of Kant, is excluded, by definition, from the political sphere, for non-resistance to violence and turning the other cheek, can only be lack of dignity when it is not saintliness. The maxim that man should not be treated as a means is incompatible with the requirements of the conquest of power. All religions have tried to resolve this conflict, especially in the most flagrant case of violence—war. Luther did it by placing the responsibility for war upon the secular power alone, and Calvin by sanctioning only wars waged for the faith. Weber seems to have been sympathetic towards the solution reached in India, where the warrior caste had a moral code sanctioning violence, politics was governed by rules of a perfect Machiavellianism, and the salvation of every individual was assured by conformity to the rules of his own caste.

Thus Weber accepted the rules of politics and chose a morality of responsibility, the only one compatible with politics and not condemned to perpetual contradictions. He violently criticized those politicians whose morality was one of pure inspiration, such as pacifists and Christian revolutionaries. He accorded to a pacifist like Förster the respect due to sincerely held convictions, while regarding the optimistic view that "from good only good can come" as puerile. As for the prophets of love, he regarded them as being condemned to simple prophecy or to the contradictory action into which for the most part they are led: that of advocating one final recourse to violence in order to establish the reign of love. Weber's acceptance of a morality of responsibility was lucid in the same way as his desire for an impartial science. In both cases, he recognized the facts of the human situation and the varieties of law appropriate to diverse activities, and aimed at establishing a relationship by careful distinction, not by compromise.

Weber's realistic political theory was intended to serve the greatness of Germany. He was certainly a nationalist. He belonged to the generation which had entered politics after the unification of Germany, and which regarded the extension of Bismarck's work as its supreme task. The unity of Germany was to be the starting-point for its role in world affairs. I do not wish to minimize Weber's nationalism, though this term usually denotes attitudes very different from his. Nothing in his writings would offend or wound a foreigner. He conceived the greatness of Germany, which was his supreme aim, less as the triumph of force than as the expansion of a civilization. In his view, the civilizations of the West had developed within the framework of great States. The Germans would be responsible before history if they allowed Russian autocracy or Anglo-Saxon pragmatism to dominate the world.

All Weber's political judgments were oriented towards this end. In internal politics he wanted to create the conditions for a world policy (*Weltpolitik*) in foreign affairs. Germany's situation seemed to him to be dominated by the conflict with Russia, the only country capable in the long run of endangering her very existence; neither England nor France constituted such a danger. Thus he was an advocate, before the first world war, of a loyal agreement with England which would make a conflict between them impossible. After Germany's defeat, he wrote, "No doubt, we have brought about the world supremacy of the Anglo-Saxons, but it was as inevitable after this war as was the supremacy of Rome after the second Punic War. There remains to us the glory of having prevented the worst: the victory of the Russian knout."

Though he was a nationalist he never lapsed into blind exaltation or demagogy; he remained ruthlessly lucid. This accounts for the dramatic character of his life. Long before the war he prophesied the catastrophe like a Jewish prophet announcing the vengeance of God. Above all he attacked the Kaiser, whose dilettantism, as it seemed to Weber, ruined everything he undertook, and whose diplomatic interventions were, at least in the form they took, indefensible and unfortunate (the Kruger telegram, the landing in Morocco). Among the Kaiser's councillors he saw no men of character; Bismarck, unable to tolerate any rivals, had created a void around himself. German diplomacy seemed to Weber to be directed by civil servants; such men only apply rules and carry out duties assigned to them, and have neither sense of initiative nor desire for power. They are, by nature, impartial and "*a*political", and are bound to carry out the orders of their superiors, whatever they may be. A politician, on the contrary, would not have accepted the Emperor's projects, for a leader feels himself responsible for what he allows to be done as well as for what he does himself. This is another form of the sense of responsibility which is characteristic of the man of action and distinguishes him from the civil servant as well as from the moralist who appeals to inspiration.

Weber, in poor health and without influence, was obliged to be a spectator of all the diplomatic errors which contributed to creating the massive coalition against Germany. He attempted, still without success, to intervene during the war; in 1915 he advocated a compromise peace, which was perhaps possible at that time. He violently opposed unrestricted submarine warfare, and in a memorandum to the Emperor he pointed out the folly of a decision to embark upon it, since it would mean the entry of America into the war, and therefore certain defeat. But despite these errors, and despite the atrocities, he accepted the war as having a purpose; he saw in it a continuation of Bismarck's work, a defence by Germany of her right to existence and to a part in world politics.

More passionately than ever he took up the question of constitutional reform, which he had been demanding long before the war. He did not expect parliamentary government to produce an immediate change or a miraculous improvement, but he hoped that it would bring about a better recruitment of leaders. At the same time he had a conception of modern politics which was free from any illusions. The bureaucratic state has become a gigantic enterprise whose operation has to be assured by civil servants, technicians and specialists. The political parties themselves are being bureaucratized, are becoming machines; with a membership devoid of ideals and blindly obeying a leader, they strive for power not so much in order to carry out a policy as to acquire places and prebends. In the state, as in the party machine, the only man worthy of the name was the leader, the Führer.

Weber, living in a world of conflicts of interest and rationalized states, had a very elevated conception of the leader. The leader, entirely devoted to his task, passionate yet lucid, is the master of his followers, and triumphs by the power of his personality, not by flattery or demagogy. He has the courage of the truth, and not merely a sense of opportunity. Weber apparently liked to reconstruct the type of the demagogue upon the model of the Jewish prophet who flays the people but nevertheless is accepted as their chief because he is endowed with exceptional virtues. The professional politician lives *from* politics, but also *for* politics. He is moved not so much by vulgar ambition as by an inner call, by a need to act and to influence men's destiny and culture. Weber was aware that his was an idealised portrait of the "charismatic" leader. But this ideal type was not so much a methodological instrument as a sketch of the type of leader he would have liked to be; his politics were heroic even more than realistic.

We may ask what was Weber's significance as a political philosopher. Should he be regarded as the "German Machiavelli", as Meinecke suggested, or as a "Heidelberg idealist" in the words of B. Groethuysen? As to his being a German Machiavelli: he held that the politician must use any necessary means, that the State is a rationalized undertaking, and that politics is a struggle for power (and for the material advantages of power). But he never said, or thought, that the end justifies *every* means, and he did not, for example, appeal to *Realpolitik* to justify the violation of Belgian neutrality.[1] Moreover, he himself declared that there are moments when the antinomy of responsibility and inspiration disappears, and when the individual has to say simply "Hier stehe ich, ich kann nicht anders". He criticized bitterly the kind of romanticism of *Realpolitik* which flourished in pre-war Germany. He denied the need to adapt oneself to

[1] He found an argument in the fact that Belgium had not fortified the frontier with France.

circumstances, in the popular sense. Though politics is the art of the possible it is often necessary to attempt the impossible in order to attain the possible. Such considerations make it necessary to qualify the attribution of Machiavellianism (at least in the popular sense of the term) to Weber's theory. In fact, they clarify the political implications of responsibility, as Weber conceived it. They remind us that this political doctrine is itself based upon a thorough-going acceptance of a cultural or human value.

Weber's philosophy is probably less contradictory than his personality. He had a conception of heroism which did not always accord very well with the actual conditions of human existence. He had a thirst for truth which was sometimes incompatible with the needs of democratic politics. Thus he had a clear idea of the right decision which a minister should have taken, but he overlooked the fact that it is first of all necessary to get into power. His attempt to convince Ludendorff that he should voluntarily give himself up to the Allied tribunals suggests a kind of heroic Utopianism. He supported his proposal by realistic arguments; for example, that genuine politics does not repudiate moral forces, and that such an act would have both an ideal and a practical significance. It is only too obvious that in this instance it was the sense of heroism rather than arguments of expediency which determined his choice. By a kind of dialectical reversal, the politician guided by a morality of responsibility is transformed into one guided by a morality of inspiration. Weber refused to employ the means necessary to obtain power. He was prepared, in the abstract, to calculate human reactions and to act in accordance with his calculations, but as a human being he refused to employ the means which he knew to be essential. He had a horror of compromise and dishonesty.

Weber's politics, which expressed a desire for lucidity, culminated in a preference for truth rather than action, and for human values rather than simple effectiveness. He accepted in theory the constraints of political action, but in practice he rejected them as soon as they threatened the dignity of the human being. He would only have accepted a position of leadership in order to raise the masses to a respect for authentic values. That is why he remained a scholar.

The contradictions in Weber's political thought are not lacking in grandeur. This nationalist had a strong feeling for the individual, supported working-class demands, and was ready to help all who suffered from collective bodies. He accepted the struggle between gods, between nations and between men, but he had a horror of a "world in which everyone swindles". Let each man choose his ideal and fight for it under its true colours. This notion of rivalry between heroes or between enlightened and lucid nations is Weber's political Utopia. His desire to distinguish clearly between what is known and what is believed, between what is desired and what is the fact, represents the scruples of an intellectual. Without these scruples he could not have lived; with them, he was unable to act.

HISTORICAL RESEARCHES

Weber's historical curiosity arises from a concern with the present; the point of origin of his researches is capitalist civilization, or rather those of its features which are unique in the history of mankind. He never loses sight of this uniqueness, which, in the last analysis, always preoccupies him and which he is trying to explain even when he is studying Buddhism or Judaism.

In the realm of knowledge only the West has developed positive science[1] combining experimentation and mathematical rigour. Only the West has developed chemistry and scientific history (as distinct from annals such as those of China), or has rationalized music and architecture to such a degree. It is only in the West that there exists a highly specialized bureaucracy composed of technical experts and jurists. In no other part of the world is there anything comparable with our constitutional states, our parliaments and political parties, and nowhere else has the legal system been rationalized to such an extent (which is a condition for stability and for exercising foresight in economic affairs). Finally, there is no equivalent in Egypt, China or the ancient world, of our bourgeois and pacific capitalism, which is based upon industrial work in rationalized enterprises, on exact calculation of costs and profits and on the separation of the enterprise and the home.

[1] Or, at least, what is to be found elsewhere in the way of positive science has no comparable development.

In one sense, therefore, the problem Weber studies is an expanded version of the Marxist problem.[1] However, to mention only the major difference, Marx saw in the society of his time a means of understanding the nature of every society and of the whole of history up to the revolution which would emancipate mankind. Western capitalist society was regarded as exemplifying in a "pure form" the constitutive social relations. It would be inaccurate to say that Marx projected into the past the present fact of class struggle, but at least, the struggle between the bourgeoisie and the proletariat was, in his view, the modern form of a conflict which existed in every society. The materialist categories were theoretically supposed to be applicable to the study of all historical periods. Weber, on the contrary, emphasizes the original features of our society, and he attempts to account for its historical uniqueness (which does not imply that it was either monstrous or accidental). Even the method of comparative sociology assumes here the significance of a philosophy of history, for the comparisons are intended to reveal the unique characteristics of Western civilization.

It would be arbitrary to relate all Weber's work to this central theme. His various studies (on the decline of the ancient world, the agrarian history of the ancient world, the money market, the condition of the worker in large-scale industry, the history of trading companies in the Middle Ages, agrarian problems of East Germany), reveal a wide-ranging curiosity, both historical and contemporary. Moreover, the range of his later work goes beyond the problems of our own civilization. Nevertheless, in a brief sketch such as the present, we may confine our attention to this central aspect of his work.

Present-day capitalist civilization, with its rationalization and its mass society, crushes the individual; it has become true that men enter into relations of production which they have not willed and under which they chafe. Yet did not other men, in the past, deliberately create, in conformity with their faith, a way of life which we are obliged to accept?[2] What is the gap between their intention and the consequences of their actions? This

---

[1] Cf. for a more detailed comparison, Löwith, 114.
[2] "Der Puritaner wollte Berufmensch sein. Wir müssen es sein". (102, I, p. 203).

question gave rise[1] to Weber's most famous study (both inside Germany and elsewhere): *The Protestant Ethic and the Spirit of Capitalism*. Its thesis, which I shall briefly outline, is well known: the Calvinist, never certain that he is one of the elect, looks for signs of his election in his earthly life, and he finds them in the prosperity of his enterprise. But he is not permitted to enjoy leisure as a result of his success, or to use his money in the pursuit of luxury or pleasure. Thus he is obliged to re-employ his money in his business, and the formation of capital takes place as a result of this ascetic obligation to save. Moreover, only regular and rationalized work, exact accounting which makes possible a knowledge of the state of the business at every moment, and pacific commerce are consistent with the spirit of this morality. For the Calvinist is master of himself, distrusts instinct and passions, is independent and has confidence only in himself, and studies and reflects upon his actions as the capitalist must do.

This theory is now so well known and has been so passionately discussed,[2] that we can rest content, for the moment, with this superficial sketch. I wish to examine more closely the methodological and philosophical import of this theory in Weber's thought. It was not at all his intention to refute Marxism by opposing to it an idealist theory of history, which indeed would have appeared to him just as schematic and indefensible as historical materialism itself. The latter was, in his view, a necessary instrument and a legitimate method of research. It is quite legitimate, so long as one is aware of the simplification involved, to study unilaterally the economic causes of historical events. Weber considered that such an intellectual division of labour had certain advantages. But he set himself against the dogmatic claim to provide a total explanation of history in terms of economic phenomena.[3] In such expressions as "real causes", applied to economic phenomena, he saw only a naïve justification of metaphysical political assumptions, without any scientific value. The economic system, far from providing the

---

[1] I do not wish to suggest that this was the psychological origin.

[2] Though historians may consider that Weber's work is out of date as regards certain matters of detail, it nevertheless retains all its interest from a methodological and theoretical point of view.

[3] I do not suggest that this was the real meaning of Marxism. I am only outlining what Weber attacked as Marxist dogmatism.

basis for an explanation of all historical phenomena, is itself not susceptible of an immanent explanation; the development of the forces and modes of production is unintelligible if other factors are not taken into account. On the other hand, Weber did not believe that "ideas rule the world"; he presented the case of Protestantism as a favourable example which enabled one to understand the way in which ideas act in history. The theological and ethical conceptions of the Protestants were influenced in their formation by various social and political circumstances, and further, they had no direct influence upon economic affairs. But ideas have their own logic, and they give rise to consequences which may have a practical influence; thus the dogmas of Calvinism, established in the consciousness of individuals belonging to particular groups, brought about a particular attitude to life and a specific form of behaviour. The individuals conformed, not simply to their self-interest, but to the internal dialectic of a system of ideas. These ideas derived their force from the acceptance by individuals of the Calvinist faith, and from the interest which they had (or believed they had) in remaining loyal to this faith. The influence of ideas is no more mysterious than that of any other motivation.

Protestantism is not *the* cause, but *one* of the causes of capitalism, or rather, it is *one* of the causes of *certain aspects* of capitalism. Here we encounter again a number of ideas which we discussed earlier; the starting-point of a search for causal relations is not a historical phenomenon such as capitalism, considered as a whole, but only certain unique features. In the case of capitalism Weber selected the characteristics which seemed to him peculiar to Western capitalism: namely, the existence of industrial enterprises with rational accounting, a rational organization of free labour, the exchange of commodities, from which resulted the separation of the enterprise from the home, and the utilization of natural science and of the technology based upon it. It is evident that the causes of capitalism will differ according to the concept of capitalism which is employed; thus for example, a different role will be attributed to the Jews and to the Protestants.

Nothing illustrates better the function of concepts in historical investigation than the controversy between Sombart and Weber about the origins of capitalism. The fundamental reason for their disagreement is that they employ different definitions of capitalism. In Sombart's work capitalism is apparently contrasted with an economic system which is primarily concerned with the satisfaction of needs (*Bedarfswirtschaft*). Capitalism is a system which is motivated by the desire for unlimited gain, and whose development has no bounds, a system characterized by exchange and money, by the concentration and circulation of wealth, and by rational calculation. These features are delineated by an intuitive grasp of the system as a whole, rather than by comparison with other civilizations.

In general, Sombart and Weber agree upon the facts and especially upon the important part played by the Jews in the development of capitalism. But Weber refused to admit that the Jews had brought about or had even contributed significantly to the formation of any of the specific features of Western capitalism. Avaricious usurers and rapacious merchants had existed in all civilizations. Commercial capitalism, and the types of capitalism represented by money-lenders, tax farmers, and war contractors, are found everywhere. But the Jews are not the creators of the specific characteristics of commerce and finance in Western civilization. They did not invent bills of exchange, stocks and shares, or the juridical forms of capitalist companies. They may have diffused them, but they did not originate them. In the development of industrial labour, on the other hand, they played no part at all. They did not create permanent, rationally organized enterprises separated from the home. Weber looks for the origins of this type of activity, at least in part, in a different ethic derived from a different religion; for there is lacking in Judaism the Puritan ideas of this-worldly asceticism and of the elect (from which it follows that success could not have any value in Judaism as a sign of divine favour). The Jew, who has different standards of morality for his co-religionists, and for those outside his religion, could not inspire complete confidence, as the Puritan did. Finally, in Judaism luxury and wealth are regarded as dangerous but are not entirely forbidden. There is no obligation to save in order to obtain salvation.

This analysis, which I have taken from a later work (105, pp.

349–51), develops the basic conception in Weber's study of Protestantism, namely, the examination of the influence of a particular belief upon behaviour. Weber establishes meaningful relationships between religious beliefs and an attitude towards life which is the conclusion men have in fact drawn from these beliefs. It is an original analysis, in the historical field, occupying an intermediate place between pure psychology and logical or theological analysis.

This meaningful relationship, or affinity, between the Protestant spirit and the capitalist spirit, does not yet constitute, in terms of the principle which we discussed earlier, a causal relation. Such a relation can only be established empirically. The ethic is not an effect of capitalism, since it can be found in situations where capitalism hardly existed. The development of capitalism can be observed in and through those social groups which accepted this ethic, and no other feature common to the groups can be discovered which might explain the phenomenon. For the further confirmation both of the evidence of a meaningful relation and of the validity of the causal connection, it is necessary to apply the rules of causal imputation which were mentioned earlier. In order to demonstrate the influence of an antecedent we have to construct a hypothetical development which would have occurred had this antecedent been absent or different. However, in the present case, we are not able to reconstruct the historical process as it might have been if the dynamic of the Protestant ethic had been lacking. Nevertheless, Weber claims to show that none of the other antecedents, and no combination of them, explains adequately the emergence of capitalism. His demonstration rests upon a series of comparisons in which he shows the consequences of these antecedents in other civilizations. At the end Weber presents his main proposition as a scientifically established truth: *Protestantism is one of the causes of modern capitalism*, or in other words, Protestantism is an antecedent whose absence would oblige us to conceive historical development as having taken a different course.

It will be seen in what respect this study is a major part of Weber's work, and in what respect it is only one part among others. Weber's historical curiosity extended to every age, and he was concerned to analyse the effects of political and social factors as well as those of religion. Nevertheless, Protestantism is a special case. An analysis of it enables us to grasp the dramatic character of history, and the paradox of consequences which are contrary to men's intentions. Protestants acquired the wealth which they condemned; like the monastic orders, they created by their asceticism that which they had rejected. We gain an insight into the gap between living ideas and ideas which have become habits or justifications. If the Puritans had, in the past, an easy conscience when they became wealthy, this easy conscience was legitimately based upon a sincerely held faith. A life of toil, aiming at profit and excluding leisure, had at that time a real significance, since it followed from a conception of the world and of God. But today, when the beliefs themselves have disappeared, is not such an attitude absurd?

Starting from the relationship between Protestantism and capitalism Weber enlarged his field of study into a comparative sociology of religion and a comparative history of capitalism. The elements of the latter study are to be found in his essays on the sociology of religion and in his book *Die Agrarverhältnisse im Altertum*. Unfortunately I cannot here examine this monumental work. Though it is primarily historical, it employs ideal type concepts and the comparative method is used to reveal the unique characteristics of the economic system of the ancient world. Weber specifies the obstacles to the emergence of a capitalist system comparable with that of our own times. Capitalism in the Roman world was essentially political and based upon slavery. This accounts for the impossibility of rational calculation, for the absence of technological progress, and for the small size of businesses. With the pacification of the Empire and the dwindling of the slave markets, Roman capitalism entered on its decline (104, pp. 289–311).

The studies in the sociology of religion (China, India and Judaism) directly continue Weber's study of Protestantism. The results confirm, in the first place, the role of Protestantism in the origins of capitalism. The confirmation is twofold: on the one hand, the other antecedents (e.g. stocks of gold, technical discoveries, law, and political organization) were not sufficient to give rise to capitalism elsewhere, and on the other hand, according to Weber, religious beliefs must be regarded, just as much as certain features of political organization, as obstacles to the development of capitalism in other civilizations. Even Confucianism, though it was primarily concerned with life in this world, and was rationalistic and economically orientated, did not lead to industrial labour. Further, by its traditionalism and by its teaching of moderation it was opposed to a capitalist economic system.

Weber did not look for causal relations in one direction only. He explains religions in the first place by the situation of the social classes which created or received them, and he then traces the consequences of the influence of religious ideas themselves. This brief statement of course involves an over-simplification, but Weber himself was obliged to simplify, since if causal relations were investigated in every direction, the investigator would lose himself in an endless enquiry. In order to limit the enquiry Weber tends to begin from the moment at which religious conceptions are formed, in order to investigate the causes of the ideas, and then to study their consequences once they have been formed.

It should be added that the study of causal relations is only a small part of these works. Even if this part were criticized or eliminated the most important would remain: namely, the analysis of different religions, not regarded as theological systems, but from the point of view of their original significance, ideological and emotional.

General Sociology

Weber's writings in this field, by their variety and originality, are difficult to bring within any usual classification. They do not belong to history (in Weber's sense), since they do not give a connected account of development or an analysis of the role of accidents. They do not belong to sociology, since there is lacking any clear attempt to generalize, except in certain places,[1] e.g. the typology of religious attitudes to the world, the caste system, and the meaning of prophecy. As Weber himself indicates, his work here is a kind of preliminary to history, or a more or less historical commentary on the sociology of religion as presented in *Wirtschaft und Gesellschaft*.

[1] Cf. 102, I, pp. 536–76.

This latter work is without question Weber's masterpiece. The aim of interpretative sociology is to "understand social action", to "explain its development and effects in causal terms". By action is meant any behaviour to which the individual attaches a meaning, and by social action is meant an act "the intention of which has reference to the behaviour of another person and which therefore is determined in its course by that behaviour".

In practice, the "intention" which should accompany an act need not be conscious; the domain of the intelligible comprises all behaviour which is intentional, i.e. which involves a combination of means in order to attain an end, or whose determining elements include at least the possibility of reasoning (in other words, all behaviour which is not an instinctive or mechanical reaction).

Since sociology aims at understanding, and since it is never satisfied with the mere establishment of a relationship, the unit beyond which it cannot go, but with which it must be concerned, is the individual. Interpretative sociology is individualistic, by virtue of a methodological postulate. Neither the body cells nor the State can be understood, since one can only understand conscious procedures and there is no consciousness other than that of individuals. Sociology can use as "data" the results of studies of race, of the influence of the physical environment, of physiological reactions and of non-interpretative psychology, e.g. psycho-pathology. But these data are only the conditions or occasions of the human acts which are the real subject matter of sociology.

Since sociology is only concerned with individual behaviour, the classification of types of action has an essential function since it determines the typology of social institutions. Weber's classification is as follows: first, action which is *zweckrational*, which combines a variety of means in order to attain ends decided upon after mature reflection; then action which is *wertrational*, which is also rational in its choice of means, but in relation to ends which have been chosen non-rationally, without concern for the consequences and without comparing them with other ends; next affective (*affektual*) action, which is determined both in its origins and in its course by sentiments; and finally traditional (*traditional*) action, which is at the extreme limit of the intelligible, and which results from habits and from established traditions.

This classification appears to have been derived, by a process of elaboration, from the theory of ideal types. The ideal type of action which is *zweckrational*, enjoys, in Weber's methodology, a certain priority in the interpretation of behaviour. The other types of action represent a new complication at each stage; first, the values are asserted by a non-rational act, then the course of the action itself is derived from sentiments, and finally there is added the non-rationality of an accepted tradition. But at the same time, this classification can also be explained in terms of interpretative psychology, in which case the types of rational, affective, and traditional action would correspond to the trilogy of society, federation and community.

On the basis of this analysis of individual behaviour Weber constructs a conceptual scheme of society as a whole. Society begins with a "social relation", that is, with the fact that individuals reciprocally orientate their behaviour to each other (a collision between two cyclists is not a social relation but the discussion which follows is). If there is a probability that such a relation will occur regularly we have either a custom, or *mores*, depending on whether the relation is due to a simple habit or to a more profound regularity. But there is social action chiefly because men have a conception of a "legitimate order". If there is a probability that violation of this order will meet with general disapproval the order is conventional; if there is a probability that violation will call forth constraint the order is juridical. The next level is that of the group (*Verband*), which is defined by the restricted or closed nature of the social relationships and by the presence of a group of individuals whose behaviour is directed toward maintaining the internal order of these relationships. Power is defined as the chance of obtaining the obedience of others to a particular command. The "power group" first appears when, within a group, some individuals have power over others; the political group is defined as a "power group" whose persistence and order are assured in a regular fashion by the use or threat of physical violence by a governing general staff (*Verwaltungsstab*). Thus without introducing any notions other than those of individual behaviour and of the interrelations between men, it is possible to establish the basic concepts.

Social relations take on the character of community or society,[1] according to whether the social relation is based upon a feeling of solidarity experienced by the individuals, or upon rational and self-interested behaviour. Social orders are distinguished in terms of the reasons which lead individuals to conform. In this way the types of action and the fundamental concepts of social relations are integrated. Both together determine the character of Weber's sociology, which establishes types rather than laws. It is a sociology which is strongly historical, and which is largely concerned with the uniqueness of Western civilisation, now conceived in still wider terms; legal rationality, the medieval town, bureaucracy, the relations between political and ecclesiastical power are analysed along with capitalist organization. The book comprises a sociology of religion, a political sociology, and a sociology of law.

The sociology of religion is, according to Weber's definition, the science of the social behaviour brought about by religion, and of the forms of religious society and community (e.g. what are the varieties of religious groups and what kind of social influence do these groups have?). Weber takes up again some of the themes of his earlier work; the conditioning of religious beliefs and practices by social classes (105, pp. 267–96), the influence of different conceptions and types of redemption upon behaviour, the varieties of religious ethics and their conflict with the world, in the economic field (interest and usury), in the political sphere (violence and war), and in the sphere of sexual relations (Christianity). Finally, he presents a systematic account of the economic ethic of the world religions. But he also expands these different themes, in the first place by using ethnographic material and by interpreting the primitive forms of religion and differentiating the types of religious group by a ditinction between priests, magicians and prophets.

Weber's sociology of law is mainly concerned with the rationalization of modern law, whose unique character is to be rational

---

[1] *Vergemeinschaftung* and *Vergesellschaftung*. It is impossible to provide an equivalent of these compound words, which refer to the "action of".

in a number of different senses: generalization, systematization, development of juridical concepts, solution of problems by the application of general principles. Weber traces throughout history the fundamental opposition between material justice which, applied directly to particular cases, corresponds to the sentiment of justice but is liable to be arbitrary, and formal legality which judges in accordance with a norm (Kadi justice and "empirical" justice). He investigates, in particular, the causes of the rationalization of modern law, analysing the influence of Roman law, of economic needs (predictable administration of law) and of political authorities, and he emphasises finally the influence of jurists, scholars and practising lawyers as a group who were (at least at one period) professionally interested in this rationalization. The latter is therefore not a direct consequence of economic development, which might have occurred without it (as indeed it did to a certain extent in England).

In Weber's political sociology the dominant concepts are those of bureaucracy, traditionalism, and charisma. The legitimation of power may be:

(1) rational, where it is based upon a belief in the legality of the rules and of leaders chosen in accordance with them.

(2) traditional, where it rests upon a belief in the sanctity of traditions and in the necessity of obeying those who are called upon to rule by those traditions.

(3) charismatic, where the subjects submit, in an exceptional emotional state, to the heroism, sanctity, or outstanding merit of an individual's personality.

These three concepts do not, of course, suffice to describe all the historical forms of power, nor are the types which they represent ever encountered in a pure form. Thus Weber develops from these types a "casuistry" of political concepts. Traditionalism, for example, may be gerontocratic, patriarchal, or patrimonial. Further, all the types serve to illuminate *one aspect* of a historical institution, so that they have to be combined in order to define a particular historical phenomenon. Thus, we may refer to a bureaucracy of a patrimonial type.

The empirical themes of political sociology are, first, the organization of these different types of power, their origins,

internal conflicts, and development (especially the "routinization" of charismatic power, the transformation of the acclaimed
leader into an elected or hereditary leader, and the transformation of his faithful companions into vassals or dependents);
secondly, the rivalry between political authorities and churches
(here Weber illumines one of the essential features of the unique
history of the West); and finally the influence of these diverse
types of political organization upon the economic system.

These brief remarks cannot give an adequate idea of the range
of Weber's book[1] in which an incomparable wealth of material is
brought together, classified, and illumined by a singular gift for
theoretical construction and comparative study. They are only
intended to indicate the framework of his research, the ideas
which directed it, and the nature of its results.

Weber's sociology is both historical and systematic, even
though it does not establish laws. The rules of regular succession
which most closely approach genuine laws would be the typical
economic relations (for example, Gresham's law) which are to
a large extent confirmed by experience. But such rules seldom
appear in *Wirtschaft und Gesellschaft*, because they refer to
behaviour of a rational type. Neither political sociology nor the
sociology of religion, nor the sociology of law present such
favourable examples. Moreover, the section of the book concerned with the economic system is primarily a sociological
theory of the economic sphere, that is, a model of the system as a
whole constructed with the aid of ideal types (similar to the
model of the social system which we discussed earlier). As to the
rules in political sociology and the sociology of religion, they
take the form of statements such as: religion facilitates the
crystallization of economic institutions; a class of warriors or of
nobles is not likely to be the bearer of a rational religious ethic,
while an oppressed class tends to adopt such religious beliefs. Or
again, a traditional system of power tends to reinforce a traditional type of economic behaviour; capitalism requires a predictable administration of justice, though it can dispense with a
rationalized legal system such as that of modern law. These
examples could be multiplied indefinitely; their purport is that

[1] I have not discussed the chapters devoted to the town, to the sociology of classes
and estates, to nations, to imperialism, etc.

the propositions formulate objective possibilities which are, according to the instances, more or less typical, more or less close to an adequate causality or a favourable action (either all oppressed classes have a particular belief, or else they have an affinity for such a belief). Weber indicates the absence as well as the presence of rules; whether charismatic power is perpetuated through transformation into regular, hereditary power, or whether it disappears with the leader's death, is decided by fortuitous events. The "routinization" of charisma is a typical development, whose forms are diverse, and which is affected by chance. In general, it is a question always of analytical relations between a certain social situation and a certain style of thought, between one institution and another, between a belief and a mode of behaviour, or between an institution and an attitude, and these relations can be both interpretatively understood and verified by reference to facts.

The notion of rationalization is the unifying element in Weber's methodology, research, and philosophy. The modern world is rationalized and divested of its charms; magicians, mystics and even philosophers have vanished. There are no longer any essences or Platonic "forms", and the scientist provides a complete explanation of cosmic phenomena with the aid of laws of mathematics and reason. The economic system is rational in its organization, in the conduct of business, in its accounting, in its search for maximum profit, and in its utilization of technology and science. Law is rational, based upon codified rules derived from general principles. Bureaucracy, in which everything is subject to rules and to exact knowledge, is rational. Religion itself, which systematizes dogma and the conditions of salvation, is rational, at least in the limited sense of rationalization on the basis of a number of non-rational presuppositions. In such conditions there is a danger of man's whole behaviour being rationalized. Both means and ends would become objects of reflection, and tradition would give way to technology and foresight. There would no longer be either munificence or spontaneity; only calculation and self-interest.

Weber could see no escape from this rationalization of human life except in a total and non-rational liberty, which he ardently claimed, but which would not be at the expense of rationalization in those areas where it was legitimate. He accepted whole-heartedly, if not joyously, the rationalization of science. He even saw the specific character of modern scientific work as being its incompleteness. Science does not reveal the innermost secret of things but explains phenomena. Thus it is continually progressing and it is the fate of every scientist to see his work surpassed. The liberty which Weber claimed was to be exercised in the political sphere against bureaucratic crystallization, and in the sphere of morality by decisions in cases of moral conflict and ultimately by a personal choice of supreme values.

Weber's contrast between knowledge and action is therefore only an instance of the more general contrast between rationalization and human liberty. His effort to distinguish clearly the respective spheres of will and knowledge is a special case of the contemporary debate between the human being and his own monstrous creations. This is a Marxist theme but Weber treats it in a different fashion. He does not believe that a political or social movement would suffice to transform our enslavement into liberty. A socialist bureaucracy would be equally burdensome and dangerous. It is the individual who must be saved. In the political sphere it was the "charismatic demagogue" who seemed to Weber a genuine individual. In the field of science and morality it was the non-rational determination of values, utilized as a frame of reference or affirmed as imperatives, which seemed to him the guarantee of personal autonomy. Finally, the struggle to dominate the blind determinism of the external world and the conflicts of irreconcilable realms of law was an activity worthy of human beings.

Max Weber, a nationalist and farsighted German, lived in the years before the first world war as a prophet of misfortune, announcing the catastrophe which he felt to be imminent. But he is not only to be understood in terms of his attitude to his own country; he was not only a German, but also a man of the twentieth century combining foresight and courage. He lived intensely our own destiny, fearful that the individual might be swallowed up by a bureaucratic apparatus, that liberty might disappear in a rational economic system, and the human person in a mass society. He represented an epoch in the history of Germany and a stage in European consciousness.

CHAPTER IV

Sociology in France and Germany

In this concluding chapter I shall try to answer the question, whether there is a German school of sociology; or at least to indicate the specific features of German sociology.

We can say, in the first place, that there is no specifically German conception of sociology; neither formal sociology, nor the sociology of knowledge can be so regarded. The problems of this latter field are well known and are a subject of discussion everywhere. As to formal sociology, the conception of sociology as an independent science, it perhaps appears less clearly in France, though it can be found in England and America. The genuine problems with which it deals belong, in Durkheimian theory, to general sociology. Finally, an "essentialist" science of society is regarded in France as being outside the domain of scientific knowledge; it is not a case, here, of the problems being ignored, but of a different philosophical approach. French positivism excludes the *Grundwissenschaft* and *Wesenswissenschaft* which phenomenology has reintroduced in Germany.

Thus the first characteristic of German sociology which we have to note is that of the philosophical trends associated with it, and the philosophical climate in which it has developed. Sombart contrasts naturalistic Western sociology with the spiritualistic German sociology (cf. 18, I p. 15). Whereas the former attempts to reduce the spiritual to the psychic, and the psychic in turn to the physiological and social, the latter, on the contrary, respects the specific nature of spiritual phenomena.

This contrast, which has often been drawn, is clearly too rigid; there is, in France a sociology based upon spiritual assumptions, while in Germany neither von Wiese nor Oppenheimer regard sociology as a *science of spirit*. The contrast can only be defended by presenting it as an opposition of "essences" and by excluding from German sociology any positivist or materialist school. Sombart does not hesitate to do this; the German "essence" is conceived by him as capable of surviving the death of all Germans, while on the other hand he asserts that Marxism does not contain a breath of the German spirit.[1]

If we reject these metaphysical assertions there remains simply the fact that German sociology tends to be spiritual while French sociology tends to be positivist. More precisely, the majority of German sociologists and the most representative of them, regard sociology as a "noological" science (in the vague sense of the term),[2] whereas Durkheim and his school regard it as a natural science. There is no equivalent in Germany of Durkheim's sociologism. Thus, although Jerusalem attempted to elaborate a sociological theory of knowledge, no bourgeois sociologist has regarded morality, religion, and value judgments as *essentially* social phenomena which can be reduced to functions of collective life.[3]

The type of German sociologism which might be compared with Durkheim's, that of Mannheim, has as its basis historical development and not collective reality; it deifies the process of development, not society. The contrast is that between Hegel and Comte, on a lower level. The "noological" character of sociology appears chiefly in the attempt to grasp the unique meaning of all human phenomena, and to distinguish carefully between *explanation* and *reduction*. The study of origins or conditions seems too often to aim at dissolving the significance of the phenomenon studied; for example, at equating the social bond with a single factor such as constraint, or at reducing religious sentiments to non-religious ones such as fear, admiration, or curiosity (or to a

---

[1] Cf. *Der proletarische Sozialismus*, 1924, pp. 81 and 85.

[2] That is to say, in the sense of the expression *Geisteswissenschaft* and not in the precise sense in which *Geist* is opposed to *Seele*.

[3] It only makes sense to refer to a phenomenon as social if one means by this *essentially* social. Since all men live in society all human phenomena are at the same time social. What has to be determined is whether they are partly, completely or essentially social; that is, consequences of collective life.

combination of such sentiments). Sociology has learned from phenomenology to distinguish the meaning of each sentiment (e.g. various forms of submission or authority), and to respect the specific character of each cultural universe. Religion, meta-physics, science and art are first of all understood in their authentic existence before the external conditions and social factors of their development are determined. Even Mannheim's dogmatic sociology respects these specific meanings, and makes them expressions of a spiritual development which is incessantly creating new forms.

Secondly, almost all German sociology uses the method of interpretative understanding. German sociologists would prob-ably all accept Weber's statement that a statistical relationship, however well established, does not satisfy our curiosity and that we desire to *understand* the link between motives and the act, which will explain human behaviour and the statistical relation itself.

It should be noted that, although such "understanding" seems incompatible with one of Durkheim's rules of method (to treat social facts as things), it is not incompatible with the actual procedure of even the most orthodox partisans of French sociology. For example, Simiand, once he has obtained the statistical data, tries to understand how the influx of gold affects economic life, and this is, at least in part, an attempt to under-stand motivated behaviour. Halbwachs, too, interprets psycho-logically his statistical correlations. Durkheim himself tried to "understand" (in Max Weber's sense) the phenomena of collec-tive life which give rise to religion, and the states of mind which lead to suicide. And Mauss writes that "the purpose of a ritual can only be found when its meaning has been discovered". Thus, this difference between French and German sociology is chiefly a matter of their programmes; French sociologists in practice use the method of "understanding" and justify it by a more or less accurate analogy with a procedure of the natural sciences. At the theoretical level the problem only emerges in discussions of the relation between sociology and psychology.

The interpretative method dispenses German sociologists from the search, or so-called search, for laws. French sociology, on the other hand, originated in a contempt for history, or at least in a desire to turn this pseudo-science into a genuine science, and sociology is therefore regarded by many as a generalizing science. Here again the contrast is mainly in the programmes; if Durkheim's work were restricted to the part which establishes laws it is doubtful whether there would be anything left (unless every statistical correlation is to be regarded as a law). This is not to say that sociology should give up the attempt to generalize, for there is at least a part of sociology which studies different civilizations and the relations between social institutions by the comparative method, and which tries to establish more or less general relations. But what is the status of these relations, and is it possible ever to arrive at laws? I only pose the question here. I have only tried to indicate that even generalizing sociology, in Germany, does not strive to imitate the natural sciences by formulating the same theoretical claims. *A fortiori*, other branches (and other schools) of sociology are unaffected by this obsession with generalization. In systematic sociology, the equivalent of the attempt to discover more and more general laws is the effort to find essential concepts and basic elements. Schmalenbach tries to determine the essential types of human groups, Vierkandt the basic sentiments, while Spann analyses the structural law of society, which is both ideal and real, since the perfect precedes the imperfect and since communities are based upon the objects of the intelligible world.

The spiritualism which pervades German sociology results in an effort to grasp the uniqueness of the cultural sciences. There are two main influences, that of Dilthey and that of phenomenology. To the former is due the notion of "understanding", and the conception of social institutions as expressions of spirit, but without any metaphysical doctrine of objective spirit or transcendental reason. The latter appears in the more or less legitimate borrowing of phenomenological procedures, such as the conceptual grasp of unanalysable wholes (Vierkandt, Spann) by a phenomenological intuition which grasps the meaning without generalizing from instances. These procedures are not, of course, adopted or even accepted by everyone. Intuition is only legitimate where it is exercised on simple elements. There is a considerable danger of arbitrariness, since it is easy to invoke intuition in order to bring analysis to a halt or to assert an essence or antithesis. There does not yet exist a social philo-sophy faithful to Husserl's teaching.

This spiritualism shows itself also in the representation of development. German sociologists do not aim to turn history into a science. They do not disregard the problems of singular causal connections, or leave out of account the possible influence of individuals. Sociology does not consist in supposing that only the masses or social situations determine events. The influence of Rickert's logic combines here with the traditional feeling for the particular. Systematic sociology, to be sure, strives to do without history. Historical sociology at least tries to distinguish itself from history, without excluding the uniqueness of develop-ment, or the reality of accidents, or the specific character of different ages. It is a historical sociology which does not claim to establish laws, or a system, or a unilinear development of mankind.

The philosophical trends which we have distinguished also find expression in the *basic concepts*. The distinctions between society and community, civilization and culture, dominate all the various schools. These concepts, at least in the sense which we have outlined, are little used in France.

Durkheim, it is true, in his review of Tönnies' book (cf. *Revue philosophique*, 1889, pp. 416-42) accepts its main conclusions (at least the analysis of community). "Society", as Tönnies described it, was in his view only a version of the industrial society dis-cussed by Spencer. But he refused to see in "society" only individualism and mechanical relations. "Society", he wrote, "is neither less organic nor less internal (than community). Besides purely individual movements there is in our contem-porary societies a truly collective activity which is just as natural as that of the smaller societies of the past." No doubt this was a just criticism; the organic and the mechanical cannot be brought together philosophically merely by juxtaposing them as the two terms of a historical development in the real world. Moreover, the life of large groups is certainly natural, if one excludes any value judgment from the notion of natural. Nevertheless Durk-heim's criticism misses the real significance of Tönnies' cate-gories. Durkheim is thinking mainly of two real social forma-tions, whereas Tönnies has in mind two ideal types, which can

be used in the analysis of any social group and not merely of a
society as a whole. Further, there is a difference in the values
emphasized. Durkheim's sympathies are with the organic
solidarity (corresponding to Tönnies' "society"), which, by the
multiplication of social circles and by contractual law, aids the
liberation of individuals. Tönnies, and especially the neo-
Romantics who use these categories, prefer the profound and
intimate union of primitive societies.

This example illustrates better than any other the extent to
which French and German sociology are close and yet remote.
Tönnies' "society" is very similar to Spencer's "industrial
society", and this in turn resembles Durkheim's "organic
solidarity". But the resonance, the significance of the terms is
quite different. The implicit criticism and the conception of
civilization which are contained in the notion of a "rational
society", vanish in the notion of "organic solidarity". They
vanish even as soon as one refers to "the truly collective action
of our modern societies", since the attention is withdrawn from
the social problem which Tönnies' antinomy discloses: namely
the nature of the relations between individuals within the collectivity, the disappearance of personal, emotional and spontaneous
bonds, and the dominance of contractual relations, of an
impersonal society and of competition.

Similarly, the terms civilization and culture, though they are
known in France, have not acquired the status of basic concepts.
The history of these two words has still to be written; their meaning has fluctuated and is still not entirely fixed. Bernheim's
Lehrbuch still attributed a moral significance to civilization (man's
self-mastery and his organization of his social relationships),
and a wider meaning to culture (deliberate human intervention
and the struggle to master nature). Nevertheless, there is a
growing agreement, at least among sociologists and historians,
to denote by culture spiritual phenomena, and by civilization
material and technological phenomena. At the same time
civilization is contrasted with culture as the older rational
societies are contrasted with younger organic societies, science
with religion, and technology with spirit.

French writers do not and cannot accept such an antithesis.
The rationalist philosopher refuses to separate science and

spirituality. And the neo-Thomist Christian will not relinquish the notion of an objective religious truth, comparable with, though superior to, scientific truth. Finally, neither the historian nor the sociologist will accept the model of the ageing of cultures; it is not in the growing rationalization of consciousness and existence that a French writer is likely to see a danger of decline. Yet it is *in opposition* to reason as it triumphs in science, in the organization of social life, and even in the individual consciousness, that culture is ultimately defined. A. Weber refers to the unexampled barbarism of our time in which society and civilization reign unchallenged, in which our egoistic impulses develop unchecked, and in which no spiritual aspiration disciplines or animates human beings. This type of sociology of culture expresses the perennial romantic protest against mechanical civilization and against science. It is inseparable from a definite metaphysic or ideology, which I will not call *essentially* German, but which is, *as a matter of fact*, widely diffused in Germany.

In other words, these two terms express, in Germany, collective representations (to use a convenient term). But the French rejection of them also reflects collective ideologies. The Comtian idea of the irreversible succession of types of knowledge, and the claim of "scientism" to possess a philosophy which is true in the same sense as natural science, appear just as self-evident in a positivist climate as do the distinction of types of knowledge which are eternally separate and equally valid, and the contrast between reason and spirit, in a romantic climate. The national character of the social sciences is related mainly to the diverse philosophies which inspire them, upon which the questions posed and the concepts employed in turn depend. Further, history is always logically (and psychologically) posterior to theory. It is in the light of a definite conception of man that the past is interpreted. Such a conception does not (or should not) alter the facts or the causal connections but it changes their significance.

It may be objected that the distinction between civilization and culture is a metaphysical one, which science ignores and should ignore. Civilization should be regarded as the whole of humanity's past acquisitions, as an intellectual and material fortune "which is shared by an ever more rational humanity", as Mauss expressed it.[1] But this formulation would be regarded by a German sociologist of the spiritual school as a sign of positivism, that is of the view that all human products are transmissible (because they are all conceived on the model of science). Perhaps unconsciously the present diffusion of the *phenomena* of *civilization* is taken to be a realization of *the* genuine civilization.

We will not pursue the methodological aspect of the problem. Metaphysical or critical concepts such as those of A. Weber cannot perhaps be employed in strictly empirical research, because they require philosophical decisions (what are the boundaries of the two spheres?) and because there is no way of testing them. It may be that certain definitions (for example, those of Mauss) can be adjudged the best in terms of the technical requirements of discovery and verification. But to judge the German sociologists in this way would be to apply a criterion which they reject. It is precisely the notion of "science" which they wish to expand, and they demand a spiritual science in order to understand the human spirit.

How should these philosophical differences be interpreted? Without even adumbrating an explanation in social terms of the different trends of French and German philosophy I should like to make one brief comment. German philosophers, especially in the nineteenth century, came largely from a background of officials, particularly church officials; the clergyman's son is the typical representative (cf. 15, pp. 3 and 53, I, p. 38). Even if they have lost their religious faith they retain a certain feeling for religion as the highest form of spiritual aspiration. They are attracted by non-dogmatic religiosity, and they distinguish science, which is objectively true, from religion, which is humanly valuable, even though it cannot be proved or refuted. This kind of religion without God leads to a recognition of the role of the emotions, which cannot be reduced to reason, and frequently inspires a protest against capitalist, rationalized society. In France, on the other hand, the direct conflict between religion and science (and philosophy) pushes both sides to make all-embracing claims which are irreconcilable with one another. Profane philosophy (or at least the most characteristic type) is

---

[1] *Civilisation: le mot et l'idée.* Première semaine internationale de synthèse, Paris 1930, p. 106.

anti-Christian, and indeed anti-religious. It is rationalist and "scientist", and rather than protesting against rationalization as such it protests against the ill use which men make of their own creations. A lengthy study would be required before these observations could be stated precisely. It may be added simply that it would be necessary first of all to study the groups which were, in France and Germany respectively, the bearers of philosophy, of science, and of religion, then the social rivalry of these groups (salons, churches, and universities), the atmosphere of the universities in the two countries, and finally the conditions in which the Romantic revival took place in the twentieth century.

Even such an account would leave unanswered two questions which may perhaps appear the most important: first, to what extent do these philosophies express a "national spirit"; and secondly, which concepts are the most useful and most fruitful in sociological enquiry? I shall not attempt even the beginnings of an answer to the first question, so obvious does it seem, and yet so impossible to demonstrate, that people express their spirit and their dispositions through their chosen ideologies. So far as the second question is concerned, it seems to me undeniable that the elements of civilization are extremely various in the case of complex civilizations. Whatever metaphysic one adopts, one is bound to recognize the variety of directions which human activity takes, and thus the multiplicity of universes in which human existence goes on. Consequently, even if civilization is defined in positivist terms, it is still necessary to distinguish other forms of thought, other reactions of man to the world. The hierarchy of functions varies, and it is necessary to distinguish between the various products and functions.

The second characteristic of German sociology seems to me to be its concern with method, its search for a philosophical basis and its uneasiness about any self-evident justification of the discipline. This has even been called a "national disease". But it is only a disease in particular circumstances; for example, in order to become a recognized teacher and to occupy a chair of sociology, the aspirant has to write a "system of sociology", and these systems often comprise nothing but methodological discussions divorced both from genuine philosophical thought and from empirical research.

Further, this desire to know oneself runs the risk of degenerating into an infinite regress of the analysis itself. The sociology of knowledge is a typical example of this "sociology of sociology" which may be, according to the use made of it, either interesting and fruitful or useless and stultifying. It is true that ethnology has a history, which is inseparable from the history of primitive societies themselves. The history of Egypt varies with the history of Egyptology, and the latter is not one of unilinear progress, of an increasing number of inscriptions deciphered, and of a more exact determination of the facts. It follows the rhythm also of the various kinds of interest which different ages have taken in Egypt. From this arises the legitimate attempt to write the history of ethnology, instead of the history of Australian societies, and to undertake the sociology of sociology instead of a sociological analysis of a particular society (in any case, the sociology of sociology is part of a sociology of the contemporary world).[1] This notion of sociology as a critical consciousness leaves no place for the idea of a single sociology, as a science whose finished structure would resemble that of physics. Under the influence of different periods, and different social classes and situations, sociology will have different points of departure and different results.

This kind of self-analysis no doubt enables each sociologist to become aware of his own standpoint, to contrast it with others, and thus to make clear its scope and limits. It aids an understanding of the nature of the social sciences, and when associated with empirical research it contributes to more lucid and profound thinking. But if it is pursued in isolation it may easily go astray. We may ask, for instance, where the analysis is to stop; why should there not be "a sociology of the history of ethnology"? After all, it is not without interest to study the circumstances in which people become aware of the characteristics of ethnology and Egyptology. Further, the method may trespass beyond its proper boundaries, if it leads to a so-called total relativism. Finally, it may lead to a neglect of difficult research, since it is easier to understand the ideas of ethnologists than those of Australian aborigines.

---

[1] It has been said that sociology is the awareness, on the part of society itself, of its internal conflicts; for example, in Germany the conflict between society and state. Cf. 113, p. 115.

As to the concern with method, it is admirable in the case of a thinker such as Max Weber, in whose work it contributed to rigour in research and to clarity in analysis. It is useful with all those who have brought to light, if they have not solved, the philosophical problems of sociology. Only if it leads to a lessening of interest in matters of fact does it become dangerous. It will seem uninteresting only to dogmatists who envisage a positivist method which is no longer "problematical", or to those who are firmly in possession of a definitive doctrine which their masters—Marx or Durkheim—have passed on.

It is, therefore, legitimate to speak of a "German sociology", though only in a limited sense. The bearing of its particular characteristics cannot be assessed on the basis of the present incomplete study. Such an assessment would, either explicitly or implicitly, form part of a general conception of the nature of sociology. We must rest content with having provided the materials with which the reader himself can make an assessment in terms of his own philosophy. In conclusion, I should like to recall, once more, that the kind of question addressed to the facts determines in large measure the kind of answer which is obtained. Philosophies of man and of history are inseparably connected with the results of sociological enquiry. The core of Durkheim's thought is the antinomy of the individual and the group; the disintegration which menaces contemporary society requires the restoration of discipline and of a collective morality. It would be easy to show the consequences of this formulation of the problem not only in Durkheim's philosophy but in the social science which he constructed. Weber's work, and that of most German sociologists, on the contrary, is concerned with the historical uniqueness of Western civilization, and with its principal feature, rationalization. Here it is a question of re-establishing a community rather than discipline, and of re-establishing it in the face of bureaucracy and an abstract social order, rather than against anarchy. The basic concepts, the historical perspectives and the methods of analysis all depend largely upon this initial assumption. Whether the divergence between French and German sociology is essential or accidental, there can be no doubt about its extent and importance.

The Problems and Methods
of Contemporary Sociology

The boundaries of the various social sciences are necessarily imprecise. We can ask what is the difference between political science and political sociology, or whether social psychology is a part of sociology. Do such phenomena as race contacts, or the interaction of productive forces and political institutions, belong to the subject matter of sociology? Such questions do not, I think, call for any dogmatic reply. The division of labour between the different disciplines is a social phenomenon which is explicable by a number of factors, as is the organization of universities themselves. It is less important to agree upon the division of the territory than to maintain an awareness of the need for co-operation between specialists and for the utilization of the various methods in conjunction with each other. Reflection on the nature of sociology has mainly a philosophical and critical bearing; it aims at clarifying the problems which arise from the attempt to study scientifically the nature and history of societies.

It has been usual to distinguish between an encyclopaedic conception in which sociology is regarded as the basic social science as well as a synthesis of the special social sciences, and a narrower conception in which sociology is only one social science among others. This distinction is convenient and pragmatically justified, but it needs to be qualified. How is the scope of sociology to be defined in terms of the second conception? By its specific method of enquiry or by the type of problems with which it deals? Let us examine the former view as developed by Professor von Wiese and his school. The *Beziehungslehre* is as modest and respectful of its own limits and of the rights of other disciplines, as encyclopaedic sociology was ambitious and imperialistic. But it is still true that von Wiese, in analysing the relations between individuals and in developing a conceptual scheme which can be utilized in all empirical research, intends to provide what may be called a fundamental theory for the social sciences, a theory of the nature of social phenomena. Now let us consider the second hypothesis, according to which sociology is defined by a circumscribed subject matter within the general field of social phenomena. We find that all the subjects of investigation which are attributed to sociology, urbanism, race contacts, social stratification, or the relations between social conditions and mental constructions (*Wissenssoziologie*), are in fact difficult to isolate, and have the character of *total* phenomena which are connected with society as a whole and with the nature of society.

Thus sociology, even when it attempts to limit its claims, does not fit easily within the bounds of a special discipline. It cannot avoid being concerned with the nature of all social phenomena and with the structure of history. Auguste Comte, who first used the word, proposed to extend scientific method to the study of social phenomena, to elucidate the meaning of the crisis in Western society, and to provide the elements of a solution or cure for this crisis by utilizing the results of scientific enquiry. Thus we can say that modern sociology had, at its origin, three aims: (i) *scientific*, to apply the methods which had been so successful in physics and biology, *mutatis mutandis* in the study of human collectivities; (ii) *historical*, to indicate the significance of the present period in the process of social development and to give an account of the history and future prospects of Western civilization; and (iii) *political*, to show that although the aim of science is to discover or understand, nevertheless a science of man cannot fail to have as a consequence, if not as an objective, the transformation of reality. The dialectical relation of knowledge and action reappears at a different level in the relation between social science and political action. Even if the scientist turns away from politics the knowledge which he spreads is still a factor influencing the environment.

These three aims are to be found in contemporary sociology as they were in that of Comte, though they are expressed today in a different form from that of positivism. Comte looked for the answers to his questions in two directions. The law of the three stages[1] indicated the stages of human thought and thus established the place of our own period in the historical process. Comte's static theory, in his system of positive philosophy, revealed the institutions which are characteristic of every human society, while his dynamics, that is, history, could only be explained with reference to human nature and to the permanent laws governing men's co-existence. Contemporary sociologists no longer nourish the hope of being able to determine so easily either the fundamental characteristics of society conceived statically, or the law which governs the development of modes of thought and thus of societies. Only the Marxists possess, or think they possess, in historical materialism, the equivalent of Comte's system; that is, a theory which enables them to understand both the structure of each society and the passage from one society to another, and upon which they can base a rational policy.

The more modest sociology of the twentieth century has not abandoned any of these three aims. Its distant goal is still a static theory, a dynamic theory, and a morality, to employ Comte's own terms. But the static theory has become a theory of social forms, more or less formalized. The dynamic theory comprises interpretations of historical development, which vary according to the interests of the thinker and the concepts used; it may become, as with Scheler, a theory of real and ideal factors. The morality is not strictly deducible from the results of scientific enquiry, because the framework of interpretation already to some extent includes value judgments, and because the facts never dictate to man what he ought to do.

A static sociology, in Comte's sense, would require a combination of psychological data (concerning the fundamental human drives), anthropological and sociological data (concerning the types of group organization which appear in every community,

[1] There is a valuable discussion of the law of the three stages in (86).

and at different historical periods), and perhaps a philosophy of existence or a moral philosophy. In fact, empirical studies do effectively bring together psychology, anthropology and sociology (and also history and economics), but they are still far from establishing the kind of supra-historical theory which Comte conceived.

The sociologists whose writings I discussed in the first chapter, under the heading of systematic sociology, do not aim so high. Their work is intended to elucidate the nature of social phenomena and to establish a number of basic concepts (society, community, federation). They differ in their conceptions of the nature of social phenomena, in their basic philosophical views (for instance, von Wiese's *relation*, Spann's *totality*), and in their methodology (in Vierkandt's case, phenomenology in a broad sense). Similarly, the three writers discussed in the second chapter, Oppenheimer, A. Weber, and Mannheim, represent three typical points of view: a sociological interpretation of historical development, a theory of the constitutive elements of development, and a theory of the relations between the social milieu and intellectual constructions.

It is, therefore, accurate to emphasise, as G. Lukacs has done in two articles on German sociology,[1] that under the Weimar Republic this sociology tended, as compared with Marxist sociology, towards formal analysis. It distinguishes supra-historical concepts from particular collectivities, does not confuse economic and social phenomena with the essential nature of epochs or peoples, establishes a distinction between judgments of fact and value judgments, and rejects the notion that an interpretation of history includes within itself either knowledge of the future or a moral imperative. If one conceives, as does Lukacs, a sociology which is both supra-historical (the eternal truth of historical materialism, of the primacy of the relations of production, etc.) and historical (the interpretation of the present and of the future to which the contradictions of the capitalist world will inevitably lead), and which is able to grasp the process of development as a whole and its meaning, then the formal analysis of Tönnies or von Wiese, the recognition of non-rational elements by A. Weber, the plurality of causal connections and the role of decision brought to light by Max Weber, are bound to

[1] *Aufbau*, nos. 5 and 6, Berlin 1945.

appear as evasions or as a descent into irrationalism. But that sociology which is the truth of history as a whole and the interpretation of the present in terms of a perfect future, exists only in Lukacs' imagination. It is not a science but a metaphysic, and a false metaphysic. For man, involved in history, is able to discover certain relations, universally true, between partial phenomena, and to discern the connections between different elements of a social structure, but he is not able to grasp the final truth of the process of development as a whole. Only the prophet believes that he soars above the world of temporal succession like God himself and understands the significance of the present time because he knows what the future will be. But prophecy is not part of science even when it calls itself materialist or camouflages itself in dialectical jargon.

From 1933 to 1945 the development of sociology was paralyzed by the National-Socialist regime. All sociology involves a questioning of the social structure and of political institutions. Thus, although even totalitarian despotism does not prohibit empirical research it can hardly tolerate an awareness, on the part of sociologists, of the present or perennial problems of society. This explains, in part, why no important reconsideration of the problems which we discussed in the first chapter has taken place.

In 1936 Vierkandt published *Familie, Volk und Staat in ihren gesellschaftlichen Lebensvorgängen: eine Einführung in die Gesellschaftslehre*, republished in 1949 under the title *Kleine Gesellschaftslehre* (to distinguish it from *Gesellschaftslehre* 1922 and 1928, which we discussed above). He employs the same method, derived from phenomenology in its broad sense, which aims at apprehending totalities, at grasping meanings, and at understanding the perpetual exchange between the life of groups themselves and the individuals who compose them (who join and leave without affecting fundamentally the whole itself).

L. von Wiese, also, continued to reflect upon the foundations and the concepts of his *Beziehungslehre*, to develop and clarify the tools of research which it offers to the sociologist, and to employ the method in numerous enquiries.[1] In the discussions concerned

[1] Cf. the symposium *Abhängigkeit und Selbständigkeit im sozialen Leben*, Cologne and Opladen 1951.

with systematic sociology three types of controversy can be distinguished. There are, first, philosophical controversies about the nature of social phenomena, and whether they should be defined in terms of relations between individuals, following von Wiese, or in terms of an apprehension of wholes or totalities, following Spann. Then there are the controversies about classification, concerned with the types of social group and the basic forms of sociability. Finally, there are methodological controversies, concerned with the appropriate methods of defining and classifying groups and of understanding collective phenomena. But it is not easy to establish a radical separation between these controversies, since philosophical orientations almost inevitably affect the selection of methods and concepts. Nevertheless, there is evident a tendency to seek a way of determining fundamental concepts independently of any particular philosophical orientation. Among the works outside Germany which illustrate this tendency may be mentioned G. Gurvitch, *La vocation actuelle de la sociologie* (Paris 1950) and the symposium edited by Talcott Parsons and E. A. Shils, *Toward a General Theory of Action* (Cambridge, Mass. 1951).

Parsons and Shils can be regarded as continuing Max Weber's attempt to construct a model of social structure and to clarify basic concepts, taking as their point of departure the notion of social action. The influence of Durkheim and Pareto is combined with that of Weber. Gurvitch opposes his theory of the basic forms of sociability and his typology of groups to the simpler classifications of von Wiese, Tönnies and Max Weber. It seems possible to distinguish more clearly, as Gurvitch has done, between the forms of sociability, the different types of group, and the types of global society or civilization. By the forms of sociability is meant the various types of collective life, such as Tönnies tried to distinguish by his concepts of society and community. Besides the form—societal or communal—which refers to the emotional intensity of collective life, or to the determining factor in the individual's participation, two other forms characteristic of all groups are indicated by the distinction between domination and collaboration.

Sociologists are still far from agreement on a general classification of groups, and the debate continues on the legitimacy or otherwise of analysing groups into more or less stable complexes of relations between individuals. It is enough to glance at the immense literature devoted to defining social class to appreciate that one of the most commonly used terms remains ambiguous. Every sociologist has his own classification of groups and employs different concepts because he refers to different criteria. A general agreement upon a single classification presupposes acceptance of the same criteria and the same methods, and this is out of the question at present as it was earlier. Despite this, it seems to me that there has been some progress in the recognition of the basic characteristics of social action and of social groups, so that the establishment of a systematic correspondence between the different classifications may not be impossible.

Rather than these theoretical studies it is the empirical investigation of small groups, and especially sociometry, which seems likely to influence the development of general sociology and especially that part concerned with the forms of sociability. It is well known that many American sociologists, among them C. H. Cooley, F. Thrasher, E. Mayo, K. Lewin, and J. L. Moreno,[1] have carried out interesting and thorough researches on small groups such as factory workshops, military formations and school classes. They have perfected a number of techniques of investigation of which the best known is sociometry. In France, G. Gurvitch has seen in the analysis of small groups, and especially in sociometry, a confirmation or illustration of his own theory of a micro-sociology applied to the deeper levels of collective life, as distinct from the macro-sociology applied to the study of large groups. Similarly, in Germany, von Wiese has taken an interest in this type of research and particularly in sociometry which seems to develop the analysis of relationships in a quantitative direction.

The sociology of small groups seems to be one of the important parts of contemporary sociology. In the study of working groups, soldiers, or school children it frequently reveals, by a sample enquiry, the causes of disturbance or equilibrium in larger groups. It is, in fact, in the small group that the individual feels himself oppressed or integrated. It would be a mistake to look

[1] See, for a valuable survey of the studies of small groups, the symposium edited by H. D. Lasswell and D. Lerner, *Political Science in the United States*.

for the origins of all social malformations at the level of small groups, but it is reasonable to consider that social crises can be observed in the sphere of micro-sociology and are at least partially explicable in terms of the relations within small groups.

These studies also have a practical bearing; they help to rectify errors in the organization of industrial work, they assist military general staffs to form harmonious units, and head teachers to create harmonious communities. But it is not this practical value which concerns us here. The study of small groups does not solve any of the theoretical problems raised by the investigation of the basic forms of sociability, but it does permit the testing of the hypotheses which theoretical work produces, and thus counters the danger of scholasticism.

Systematic sociology, as the branch of general sociology concerned with the principles and concepts utilized in all the special sociologies, will always retain the complexity which results from the intermingling of philosophical, methodological and conceptual discussions. But it is enriched and fertilized by the experimental study of the basic groups which underlie all social groups, from the smallest to the largest, in all periods and under all regimes.

The work of A. Weber and of K. Mannheim was by no means at an end when the first edition of this book appeared. Mannheim, who settled in Great Britain where his ideas had a considerable influence, published *Mensch und Gesellschaft im Zeitalter des Umbaus* (Leyden 1935) and *Diagnosis of our Time* (London 1942), while A. Weber published, before the second world war, his *Kulturgeschichte als Kultursoziologie* (Leyden 1935), and after the war *Das Tragische in der Geschichte* (Hamburg 1945) and *Abschied von der bisherigen Geschichte* (Hamburg 1946).

Mannheim, in his later writings, extended the range of his enquiries. He devoted less thought to the theme of the relation between the social milieu and intellectual constructions, and turned his attention to contemporary society and its crisis. In his later years he was concerned with two main problems: first, how freedom could be safeguarded in societies which would inevitably be subjected to an increasing degree of planning, and secondly, what kind of religious sentiments could invigorate spiritual life and maintain a moral consensus, beside or above the traditional religions, whose adherents are, in our societies, only a minority of the population. Oddly enough, A. Weber, who came from a totally different social and intellectual milieu, arrived in his later works at very similar speculations. He also, reflecting upon the contemporary crisis, sought in spiritual, quasi-religious affirmations (though outside any orthodox doctrine) a surer way of overcoming nihilism. This quasi-religious feeling which finds expression in the philosophy of Schopenhauer and Bergson, and in the works of poets and mystics, Dante and Shakespeare, was to be associated with liberal political institutions, with more or less socialist economic institutions, and with an international regime in which the perennial rivalry of states would be limited if not eliminated.

Thus, in their later works, Mannheim and A. Weber gave back to historical sociology the orientation which it had at first; namely, the interpretation of the crisis of Western societies. In the last few years there have been many books on this theme, of which I will mention only K. A. Fischer, *Kultur und Gesellung* (Cologne and Opladen, 1950). The author attempts to provide for the sociology of culture the kind of conceptual scheme which Max Weber's followers have tried to elaborate for the sociology of social action and social groups.

These diagnoses of the sickness of our age have been provoked by events themselves, and certain features of the development of industrial societies, in particular, have given rise to new formulations of the problems of historical sociology. At the end of the nineteenth and beginning of the twentieth century there was vigorous discussion, in both Marxist and anti-Marxist circles, of the extent to which Marx's predictions conformed with the actual course of events. In general, Marx's predictions were equated with the popular versions of the theory of capitalist concentration, of the increasing severity of crises, and of "proletarianization" and pauperization. Bernstein had little difficulty in showing that small and medium property was not disappearing in the sphere of agriculture, and that the middle classes were not being eliminated or thrust down into the proletariat. Revisionism was solemnly condemned in the socialist congresses of the early years of the twentieth century, while many non-

Marxist sociologists had adopted the conceptions of the revisionists but without elaborating their own theory of capitalist development. So far as non-Marxist sociologists ventured upon interpretations of historical development they were more inclined to emphasize such phenomena as mass society and rationalization than the broad features of economic, social and political development. At the present time, it seems to me, sociology is gradually elaborating what might be termed a *theory of the development of industrial societies*.

I deliberately use the term "industrial societies", and not "capitalist societies", since the basic phenomenon, the primary factor, is not that of the private or public ownership of the means of production, or even the relative extent of a market economy and economic planning. Perhaps private property, the market, and intellectual freedom were necessary to the emergence of industrial society, that is, to the application of science to production, the revolution in agricultural methods and the invention of machines. But once the state of mind and the instruments of industrial society have been created, this society can develop just as well with a system of public ownership and economic planning as with a system of private ownership and competition, as the example of Soviet Russia proves.

In *The Conditions of Economic Progress* (2nd edn. London 1951) Colin Clark has worked out, on the basis of statistical information, a theory of economic progress which is, to a great extent, equally applicable to societies of the Soviet type as to liberal societies. The principal elements, according to this theory, are an increase in the productivity of labour, the transfer of labour from the primary sector (agriculture and extractive industries) to the secondary sector (transformation industries) and afterwards to the tertiary sector (commerce, transport, finance and luxury trades), the complete satisfaction of primary needs which allows labour and resources to be devoted to the satisfaction of secondary needs, and when these are satisfied, the transfer of effort to the tertiary sphere, which however is marked by negligible technological progress and by the insatiable character of needs.

This model of economic development, which Colin Clark

first outlined, and which Fourastié[1] in France has elaborated and modified, indicates the results of economic history rather than the factors or the human vicissitudes of this history. In what ways did the transfer of labour from the primary to the secondary industries take place? What forces compelled individuals to make the change, and how quickly and with what accompanying misery was it effected? There are great variations from one country to another. Different countries have progressed unequally along the road of industrial civilization, that is, of increasing productivity, of a larger national income and of a redistribution of the working population. Moreover, between countries at the same level of productivity, and at the same stage in the development of industrial society, there are differences in the relative importance of agriculture and the transformation industries, depending on the geographical environment and political circumstances. The degree of inequality, the standard of life, and the rate of capital accumulation will vary according to the political regime.

J. A. Schumpeter has analysed, in *Capitalism, Socialism and Democracy* (New York 1942) the changes in capitalist economy, that is, in an economy based upon private property and market competition. His book provides a wealth of ideas and facts about the concentration of industry, the role of trusts, the function of the pre-capitalist social and political hierarchy as a protective framework for the emerging industrial society, and the changes in modes of thought and ideologies necessary to the survival of capitalism.

A recent book by J. K. Galbraith,[2] which is less scientific than those we have discussed, but which has many illuminating insights, analyses the working of competition in the U.S.A. The author shows how widely this diverges from the analytical model of classical economics, which assumed the existence of a large number of independent producers, none of whom could by himself change the market situation. He shows that in the U.S.A. the economic system is a balance of power in which no single power is able to dominate the system entirely, to such an

---

[1] See especially, Jean Fourastié, *Machinisme et bien-être*, Paris 1951; also *Le grand espoir du XXᵉ. siècle*, Paris 1949, and *L'économie en 1960*, Paris 1947.
[2] J. K Galbraith, *American Capitalism*, Boston 1952.

extent that a manufacturing trust or a small group of huge industrial concerns dominating a particular sector are confronted by buyers who are equally well organized and who can bargain on a footing of equality.

Though there is still controversy about the economic development of Western countries, a number of its main characteristics and especially the social changes accompanying industrial development, are well established. These changes have been studied almost exclusively in Western societies because of the absence of adequate information about societies of the Soviet type; this is regrettable, for it would be of the greatest interest to compare, for example, social stratification in a Soviet regime with that in a Western society at the same level of industrial development. Two recent books[1] have discussed social stratification in Western societies and have made a notable contribution to the study of its changing character.

The broad results of these studies, which I shall not attempt to summarize since their validity rests upon a precise and refined analysis, are to show that the thesis of increasing pauperization (whether in its popular or more subtle presentation) is entirely false. The standard of life of the population as a whole, including the working class, rises steadily with increasing productivity. The working class does not grow in numbers or in homogeneity by the absorption of other social groups, but on the contrary, there is increasing social differentiation. The numbers in the intermediate groups do not decline; the small producers— peasants, shopkeepers and small businessmen—hold their own, though with greater or lesser difficulty in different countries. The struggle between the working class and the employers tends to become less acute, as workers begin to share in the improvements in the standard of life, and as the struggle itself is institutionalized and the trade unions become a recognized power in society. At the same time the development of the tertiary sector of the economy continually increases the numbers of clerical workers, technicians, civil servants, etc.

The study of social stratification helps to explain a number of characteristics of the present age. There are, in all industrial

[1] René König, *Soziologie heute*, Zurich 1949; Theodore Geiger, *Die Klassengesellschaft im Schmelztiegel*, Cologne and The Hague 1949.

societies, non-proletarian masses, whose political behaviour is not economically determined. Social classes themselves no longer have such clear-cut boundaries, or such conscious and deliberate collective aims, for the state to be defined in terms of a ruling class. The state is not simply a function of the economically dominant class, nor is it always controlled by a single and united group. One of the leading ideas of Italian writers such as Mosca, Pareto and Michels, who have perpetuated in the present century the tradition of Machiavelli, is that of a dominant minority which monopolizes power, and which is distinguishable from the mass of the governed. More recently, James Burnham, in *The Managerial Revolution* has presented the managers, the officials who are responsible for the operation of large-scale administration both public and private, as an emerging ruling class which will, in all the various social systems, gradually take over power. It is probably better to speak of ruling groups than of a ruling class, and to study the various minorities —politicians, managers, civil servants, owners of the means of production, leaders of the masses, and intellectuals—which exist in all Western societies, but which are interrelated in different ways in different regimes. In democratic societies they accept a condition of permanent rivalry among themselves, while in totalitarian societies they are subjected to the decisions of a single minority group.

Max Weber regarded the mode of recruitment of leaders as a highly important feature of any political system, and he contrasted the bureaucratic recruitment in the German Empire with recruitment by parliamentary rivalry. The subject is important and wide-ranging. What is the quality of recruitment in mass parties and in parties of notables? What type of individual is generally successful in the semi-bureaucratic competition within the parties? What type of individual is successful in an organized parliamentary system such as that of Great Britain, and in an anarchic parliamentary system such as that of France? But a detailed analysis would go beyond this examination of the relations between the mode of recruitment and the type of successful individual, to study the permanent relations between the various ruling groups—managers, owners of the means of production, leaders of the masses, and politicians—which define a social and political system. If it is merely asserted, as in the jargon of vulgar Marxism, that the U.S.A. is ruled by the bourgeoisie, while the U.S.S.R. is ruled by the proletariat, sociology remains at the scientific level of Aristotelian physics. We need to ask who are the managers in the U.S.A. and the U.S.S.R., how they are recruited, and how they are related to political leaders and to the state. What are the real relationships, in the U.S.A., between the managers of large enterprises, civil servants, and politicians, and what forms does the conflict between employers' associations and industrial or agricultural trade unions take? And in the U.S.S.R., what is the character of the competition between parties, the police, the administration and the army?

Thus one is led from the study of social stratification to the study of ruling classes and of the nature of the state. This is perhaps the greatest difference between contemporary sociology and the sociology of twenty years ago. We have all become intensely aware of power as the major phenomenon in all societies, and as a problem which no reforms in the property system or in the functioning of the economy can solve. It is true that Max Weber never wearied of emphasizing the nature of power as a demoniac force from which it was impossible to escape. But in our own time power—that is, the state as the source of the authority which a few individuals exercise over their fellows—appears to the observer in more hideous and terrifying forms.

Ten years ago an important book on this subject was published by a French writer.[1] More recently, a German sociologist has taken the same phenomenon of power as the starting point for reflection on the philosophy of history. A. Rüstow's book, which is to appear in three volumes, of which two have so far been published,[2] is clearly an important work. One of its leading ideas, that the hierarchy of classes can be traced back to the wars between peoples with different ways of life—hunters and pastoralists, nomads and sedentary peoples—already has a long history in sociological literature. The range of the work, its erudition and its political importance, are alike evident. Rüstow, like A. Weber, whose successor he is at the University of Heidelberg, orientates his historical and critical study of culture toward

---

[1] Bertrand de Jouvenel, *Du Pouvoir*, 2nd edn. Geneva 1947.
[2] A. Rüstow, *Ortsbestimmung der Gegenwart*, Zurich, Vol. I, 1950, Vol. II, 1952.

the values of political and intellectual liberty and man's accomplishment of his spiritual vocation.

The classical themes of the origins of the social hierarchy, the functions of war, and racial differences between rulers and ruled, find a place among the problems of contemporary sociology, for reasons which the tragic events of the last twenty years explain. It is totalitarianism, as the principal phenomenon of our age, which obsesses the minds of sociologists. The book by Mrs Hannah Arendt,[1] who is an American citizen but who was educated in the German universities of the Weimar period, is an important contribution to the sociology of totalitarianism. The author does not quite succeed in convincing us that there is a straightforward development from Austrian and French anti-Semitism, through British Imperialism, to National Socialism and Stalinism. Despite its title the book throws more light on the nature than on the origins of totalitarianism; and in particular, the chapters concerned with propaganda, the police, and terror, seem to touch the most important features of the phenomenon. The historical developments of modern Europe—the crises of nation-states, the weakening of parliamentary regimes, the disintegration of those societies in which social classes still had some of the characteristics of estates, and the emergence of urban masses—all seem to lead in the direction of totalitarianism. These crises favour the appearance of political parties which claim a monopoly of power, which are organized on authoritarian lines, and which spread the cult of the leader and propagate a doctrine claiming to be scientific but characterized by a religious fervour. Once successful, these parties instal a permanent revolution from above, in order to mould reality in accordance with their ideas and to enforce conformity upon all individuals and groups in society. They are obliged, in order to maintain themselves in power and to approach their ideal, to make use of terror and a political police, and these finally become an integral part of the system.

This sociology of contemporary political systems overlaps with the sociology of culture and cultural crises. One is inclined

[1] Published in the U.S.A. under the title *Origins of Totalitarianism*, New York 1951, and subsequently in Great Britain under the title *The Burden of our Time*, London 1952.

to say that the contemporary themes of historical sociology derive from Comte's concern for spiritual values in a scientific age, from de Tocqueville's fear that egalitarian societies would become tyrannical, and from Burkhardt's vision of a mass society, as much as from Marx's work. Marx believed that power was a function of economic dominance, that culture was always that of the ruling class, and that the revolution which was to eliminate the bourgeoisie, socialize the means of production and give power to the proletariat, would ensure the future development of culture. Neither the nineteenth-century German historians, nor Nietzsche or Burkhardt, Alfred Weber, Mannheim or Max Weber, subscribed to these simple and over-optimistic beliefs. But it is now possible to show from experience the errors of this kind of prediction.

By comparing the development of industrialism in various environments it is possible to distinguish between those features which are necessary to every industrial society and those which are the result of pre-industrial traditions or of local circumstances. For example, if two societies at the same stage of industrial development (England in the first half of the nineteenth century and the U.S.S.R. in the first half of the twentieth century) are compared, it is possible to see which phenomena result from the economic stage reached and which are explicable in terms of historical traditions and the techniques employed. The fact that different societies, at the same level of industrial development, have had quite different political regimes, shows that economic factors do not determine political institutions in a uniform way, or at least, that the economic system is only one factor among others. Economic development entails a number of changes in social stratification, and these changes in turn facilitate certain political trends. The relations between ruling groups which industrial development brings about are not determined uniformly by the level of productive forces or by the relations between classes, but by very complex forces which include the behaviour of the ruling minorities, the ruling ideologies, and the activities of intellectuals.

So far as the political sphere is concerned one is inclined to say that contemporary economic and social conditions are almost irresistibly favourable to the growth of power, but that they do not entail a total or totalitarian state. Similarly, a mass civilization with its expanding towns, and its multiplication of media of communication such as the press and radio, is inevitable, but it is not necessary to accept as inevitable all the institutions supposedly appropriate to the age of the masses. Men still retain a sphere of liberty.

When I first made this study twenty years ago I emphasized some of the national characteristics of German sociology. At the present time I should be less inclined to do this, because, although these characteristics are real, they seem less important than the borrowings which have taken place between the various national schools. The victory of National Socialism in Germany led to the emigration of some of the most eminent representatives of German sociology, which thus spread its influence abroad during the period in which it was being repressed in its own country. Mannheim in England, Geiger[1] in Denmark, and numerous scholars in the U.S.A., at the *New School of Social Research*, and especially the *Institut für Sozialforschung* under the direction of Max Horkheimer[2] in New York and Paris, helped to spread the ideas, concepts and problems characteristic of German sociology.

The sociology which has, during the past few years, made a welcome reappearance in Germany, is quite clearly connected with the sociological tradition whose main features I have analysed. But it has received many useful external influences, just as it has contributed in many ways to sociological enquiry in other countries. In the present chapter I have referred indiscriminately to German, French and American writings, because in fact they reveal the same preoccupations, discuss the same problems, and have their place in a single intellectual movement.[3] The similarities appear just as strongly in research methods. American techniques of investigation are widely used. Inten-

[1] Geiger's principal works were: *Die Masse und ihre Aktion*, Stuttgart 1926; *Die soziale Schichtung des deutschen Volkes*, Stuttgart 1932; *Aufgaben und Stellung der Intelligenz in der Gesellschaft* (first published in Swedish), Stuttgart 1949; *Die Klassengesellschaft im Schmelztiegel*, Cologne and The Hague 1949.

[2] The *Zeitschrift für Sozialforschung* was published in Paris, 1934–37. The symposium *Autorität und Familie*, Paris 1936, was primarily the work of members of the Institute. See also M. Horkheimer and T. W. Adorno, *Dialektik der Aufklärung*, Amsterdam 1946, and M. Horkheimer, *Eclipse of Reason*, New York 1947.

[3] This is brilliantly shown in M. Horkheimer (ed.) *Survey of the Social Sciences in Germany*.

sive interviews, public opinion surveys, questionnaires, and social survey methods (especially urban surveys) as they have been so successfully used in Great Britain, are now regularly employed by German sociologists. The social conditions resulting from the war have stimulated research especially on the family, on young people (particularly the refugees from the Eastern zone and in Berlin), and on the attitudes inherited from the Nazi period. It is not often that a country has presented such a wealth of material for sociological investigation, or that the interest and curiosity of sociologists have been so lively as in contemporary Germany. The present crisis, the conflict between the liberal democracies and the Soviet regime, which for the time being divides Germany into two zones, the memories of National Socialism, the uncertainties of the restored parliamentary institutions, and the reflections upon industrial civilization, all conspire to attract the attention of the philosopher, the historian and the social student. It is the business of the sociologist to combine the concern of the first of these with the knowledge of the second and the patience of the third, and to unite their virtues in a striving for objective and verifiable knowledge.

Sociology, in all countries, is advancing towards this synthesis, to which German sociology can contribute a unique philosophical tradition as well as justifying anew the commonplace and cruel observation that historical misfortunes encourage the development of the social sciences. Sociology, which originated in a philosophical ambition, but which aims at scientific rigour, should be able to profit, more than any other discipline, from a historical situation in which man has lost the certitudes which he believed unassailable and must create his own individual life within a collectivity whose destiny opens upon the unknown.

Selected Bibliography

This bibliography has been revised by the author. A number of the original items have been deleted and in order not to alter references in the text throughout, the original numbers of the remaining books have been retained.

I. INTRODUCTORY WORKS

1. Simmel, Georg, *Grundfragen der Soziologie* (*Individuum und Gesellschaft*), Berlin, 1917.
2. Wiese, Leopold von, *Soziologie, Geschichte und Hauptprobleme*, 2nd edn., Berlin, 1931 (4th edn., 1950).
3. Freyer, Hans, *Einleitung in die Soziologie*, Stuttgart, 1931.
4. Tönnies, Ferdinand, *Einführung in die Soziologie*, Stuttgart, 1931.
5. Menzel, Adolf, *Grundriß der Soziologie*, Baden bei Wien and Leipzig, 1938.

II. GENERAL WORKS

11. *Handwörterbuch der Soziologie*, edited by Alfred Vierkandt, Stuttgart, 1931.
12. Barth, Paul, *Die Philosophie der Geschichte als Soziologie, Grundlegung und kritische Übersicht*, 3rd and 4th edn., Leipzig, 1922.
13. Sorokin, Pitirim, *Contemporary Sociological Theories*, New York and London, 1928.
14. Abel, Theodore, *Systematic Sociology in Germany*, New York, 1929.
15. Oppenheimer, Franz, *Richtungen der neueren deutschen Soziologie*, Jena, 1928.
16. *Soziologie von heute, ein Symposion der Zeitschrift für Völkerpsychologie und Soziologie* (with contributions from A. Walther, H. Freyer, J. Plenge, P. A. Sorokin, M. Ginsberg, W. F. Ogburn, R. M. MacIver, S. R. Steinmetz, F. Tönnies, R. Thurnwald), Leipzig, 1932.

17. *Verhandlungen der deutschen Soziologentage*, Tübingen 1910-1948 (since 1948 in the *Kölner Zeitschrift für Soziologie*).
18. *Erinnerungsgabe für Max Weber, Hauptprobleme der Soziologie*, Leipzig, 1923 (2 Vols.).
19. *An Introduction to the History of Sociology*, edited by Harry Elmer Barnes, Chicago, 1948.
20. *Soziologie und Leben, die soziologische Dimension der Fachwissenschaften*, edited by C. Brinkmann, Tübingen, 1952.
21. Schoeck, Helmut, *Soziologie, Geschichte ihrer Probleme*, Freiburg and Munich, 1952.

III. SYSTEMATIC SOCIOLOGY

25. Simmel, Georg, *Über soziale Differenzierung, Soziologische und psychologische Untersuchungen*, New impression, 1905.
26. Simmel, Georg, *Philosophie des Geldes*, 2nd edn., Leipzig, 1907.
27. Simmel, Georg, *Soziologie, Untersuchungen über die Formen der Vergesellschaftung*, Leipzig, 1908.
28. Spykman, J., *The Social Theory of Georg Simmel*, Chicago, 1925 (includes a bibliography of Simmel's works).
29. Wiese, Leopold von, *System der Soziologie als Lehre von den sozialen Prozessen und den sozialen Gebilden der Menschen (Beziehungslehre)*, 2nd enlarged edn., Munich, 1933.
30. Wiese, Leopold von, *Homo sum*, Jena, 1940.
31. Wiese, Leopold von, *Ethik in der Schauweise der Wissenschaften vom Menschen und von der Gesellschaft*, Berne, 1947.
32. Wiese, Leopold von, *Gesellschaft, Stände und Klassen*, Munich, 1950.
33. *Studien zur Soziologie. Festgabe für L. v. Wiese aus Anlaß der Vollendung seines 70. Lebensjahres*, edited by L. H. A. Geck, J. v. Kempski, H. Meuter, Mainz, 1948.
34. *Soziologische Forschung in unserer Zeit, ein Sammelwerk Leopold von Wiese zum 75. Geburtstag*, edited by K. G. Specht, Cologne and Opladen, 1951.
35. *Kölner Vierteljahrshefte für Soziologie* (1921-1933) and *Kölner Zeitschrift für Soziologie*, new series of the *Kölner Vierteljahrshefte für Soziologie*, edited by L. v. Wiese (1948 ff.).
36. *Abhängigkeit und Selbständigkeit im sozialen Leben*, edited by L. v. Wiese, Cologne and Opladen, 1951.
40. Tönnies, Ferdinand, *Gemeinschaft und Gesellschaft*, 6th and 7th edn., Berlin, 1926.
41. Leemans, V., *Tönnies et la sociologie contemporaine en Allemagne*, Paris, 1934 (includes a bibliography of Tönnies' works).

138 GERMAN SOCIOLOGY

42. Schmalenbach, Hermann, "Die soziologische Kategorie des Bundes", in *Dioskuren* (Vol. I), Munich, 1922.
46. Vierkandt, Alfred, *Gesellschaftslehre, Hauptprobleme der philosophischen Soziologie*, 1st edn., Stuttgart, 1923. 2nd revised edn., Stuttgart, 1928.
47. Vierkandt, Alfred, *Familie, Volk und Staat in ihren gesellschaftlichen Lebensvorgängen*, Stuttgart. 1936, 2nd edn. with the title *Kleine Gesellschaftslehre*, Stuttgart, 1949.
48. *Gegenwartsprobleme der Soziologie, Alfred Vierkandt zum 80. Geburtstag*, Potsdam, 1949 (includes a complete bibliography of Vierkandt's works).
51. Spann, Othmar, *Gesellschaftslehre*, 2nd edn., Leipzig, 1923.
52. Wagner, H. G., *Essai sur l'universalisme économique. Othmar Spann.* Paris, 1931 (includes a bibliography of Spann's works).

IV. HISTORICAL SOCIOLOGY

53. Oppenheimer, Franz, *System der Soziologie* (I. Allgemeine Soziologie; II. Der Staat; III. Theorie der reinen politischen Ökonomie; IV. Rom und die Germanen; V. Bauern und Städter), 1923–26–29–33–35.
56. Weber, Alfred, "Prinzipielles zur Kultursoziologie", in *Archiv für Sozialwissenschaft und Sozialpolitik*, Vol. 55.
57. Weber, Alfred, "Kultursoziologische Versuche. Das alte Ägypten und Babylon", in *Archiv für Sozialwissenschaft und Sozialpolitik*, Vol. 55, 1926.
58. Weber, Alfred, *Ideen zur Staats- und Kultursoziologie*, Karlsruhe, 1927.
59. Weber, Alfred, *Kulturgeschichte als Kultursoziologie*, Leiden, 1935, 2nd enlarged edn., Munich, 1950.
60. Weber, Alfred, *Das Tragische in der Geschichte*, Hamburg, 1943.
61. Weber, Alfred, *Abschied von der bisherigen Geschichte*, Hamburg, 1946.
62. Weber, Alfred, *Prinzipien der Geschichts- und Kultursoziologie*, Munich, 1951.
63. Fischer, K. A., *Kultur und Gesellung*, Cologne and Opladen, 1950.
64. *Synopsis, Festgabe für Alfred Weber*, Heidelberg, 1948. See particularly: E. W. Eschmann, "A. Webers metaphysische Position".
66. Rüstow, Alexander, *Ortsbestimmung der Gegenwart*, Zürich, Vol. 1, 1950, Vol. 2, 1952.
67. Spengler, Oswald, *Der Untergang des Abendlandes, Umrisse einer Morphologie der Weltgeschichte*, Munich, 1918 and 1922.

68. Frobenius, Leo, *Paideuma*, Frankfurt, 1928.
71. Mannheim, Karl, "Historismus", in *Archiv für Sozialwissenschaft und Sozialpolitik*, Vol. 54, Tübingen, 1925.
72. Mannheim, Karl, "Das Problem einer Soziologie des Wissens", ibid., Vol. 54, 1925.
73. Mannheim, Karl, "Das konservative Denken", ibid., Vol. 57, 1927.
74. Mannheim, Karl, "Die Bedeutung der Konkurrenz im Gebiete des Geistigen", *Verh. des 6. dt. Soziologentages*, Tübingen, 1929.
75. Mannheim, Karl, *Ideologie und Utopie*, Bonn, 1929. New edn. with a preface and additional chapter, Bonn, 1952.
76. Mannheim, Karl, *Die Gegenwartsaufgaben der Soziologie*, Tübingen, 1932.
77. Mannheim, Karl, *Mensch und Gesellschaft im Zeitalter des Umbaus*, Leiden, 1935. English edn., London, 1940.
78. Mannheim, Karl, *Diagnosis of our Time*, London, 1943; in German *Diagnose unserer Zeit*, Zürich, 1951.
79. Mannheim, Karl, *Freedom, Power and Democratic Planning*, London, 1951.
83. Bogdanoff, A., *Die Entwicklungsformen der Gesellschaft und die Wissenschaft*, Berlin, 1924.
84. Lukàcs, Georg, *Geschichte und Klassenbewußtsein*, in: "Kleine revolutionäre Bibliothek", Vol. 9, Berlin, 1923.
85. Adler, Max, *Lehrbuch der materialistischen Geschichtsauffassung*, Vol. I and II. Berlin, 1930–32.
86. Scheler, Max, *Die Wissensformen und die Gesellschaft*, Leipzig, 1926.
87. Scheler, Max, *Die Formen des Wissens und die Bildung*, Bonn, 1925, new edn. with the title *Bildung und Wissen*, Frankfurt, 1947.
88. Schelting, Alexander von, "Zum Streit um die Wissenssoziologie", in *Archiv für Sozialwissenschaft und Sozialpolitik*, Vol. 62, 1929.
89. Grünwald, Ernst, *Das Problem der Soziologie des Wissens*, Vienna and Leipzig, 1934.
90. Barth, Hans, *Wahrheit und Ideologie*, Zürich, 1945.
91. Geiger, Theodor, "Kritische Bemerkungen zum Begriff der Ideologie", in *Gegenwartsprobleme der Soziologie* (Vierkandt-Festschrift, 1949).
92. Lieber, Hans-Joachim, *Wissen und Gesellschaft, die Probleme der Wissenssoziologie*, Tübingen, 1952.
93. Martin, Alfred von, *Geist und Gesellschaft, soziologische Skizzen zur europäischen Kulturgeschichte*, Frankfurt, 1948.

94. Horkheimer, Max, and Adorno, Theodor W., *Dialektik der Aufklärung*, Amsterdam, 1946.

95. Adorno, Theodor W., *Minima Moralia, Reflexionen aus dem beschädigten Leben*, Frankfurt, 1951.

V. MAX WEBER

101. Weber, Max, *Gesammelte Aufsätze zur Wissenschaftslehre*, Tübingen, 1922.

102. Weber, Max, *Gesammelte Aufsätze zur Religionssoziologie*, 3 Vols. Tübingen, 1921.

103. Weber, Max, *Gesammelte Aufsätze zur Soziologie und Sozialpolitik*, Tübingen, 1924.

104. Weber, Max, *Gesammelte Aufsätze zur Sozial- und Wirtschaftsgeschichte*, Tübingen, 1924.

105. Weber, Max, *Wirtschaft und Gesellschaft, Grundriß der Sozialökonomik*, III. Abteilung, Tübingen, 1925.

106. Weber, Max, *Gesammelte politische Schriften*, Munich, 1921.

107. Weber, Max, *Wirtschaftsgeschichte, Abriß der universalen Sozial- und Wirtschaftsgeschichte*, Munich, 1923.

108. Weber, Max, *Schriften zur theoretischen Soziologie, zur Soziologie der Politik und Verfassung*, with an introduction and notes by Max Graf zu Solms, in the series "Civitas Gentium", Vol. I. Frankfurt, 1947 (includes a bibliography of writings of and about Weber).

109. Weber, Max, *Aus den Schriften zur Religionssoziologie;* selected writings with an introduction and notes by Max Ernst Graf zu Solms, in "Civitas Gentium", Vol. II. Frankfurt, 1948 (with a critical introduction).

110. Schelting, Alexander von, "Die logische Theorie der historischen Kulturwissenschaft von Max Weber und im besonderen sein Begriff des Idealtypus", in *Archiv für Sozialwissenschaft und Sozialpolitik*, Vol. 49, 1922.

111. Schelting, Alexander von, *Max Webers Wissenschaftslehre*, Tübingen, 1934.

112. Meinecke, Friedrich, "Drei Generationen deutscher Gelehrtenpolitik", in *Historische Zeitschrift*, Vol. 125.

113. Mises, L. von, "Soziologie und Geschichte, Epilog zum Methodenstreit in der Nationalökonomie", in *Archiv*, Vol. 61, 1929.

114. Löwith, Karl, "Marx und Max Weber", in *Archiv für Sozialwissenschaft und Sozialpolitik*, Vol. 67, 1932.

115. Honigsheim, Paul, "Max Weber als Soziologe", in *Kölner Viertel-jahreshefte für Soziologie*, I, 1921. "Der Max-Weber-Kreis in Heidelberg", ibid., V, 1926.

116. Jaspers, Karl, *Max Weber, deutsches Wesen im politischen Denken, in Forschen und Philosophieren*, Oldenburg, 1932.

117. Oppenheimer, Hans, *Die Logik der soziologischen Begriffsbildung mit besonderer Berücksichtigung von Max Weber*, Tübingen, 1925.

118. Walter, A., "Max Weber als Soziologe", in *Jahrbuch für Soziologie*, Karlsruhe, 1926, Vol. II.

119. Schütz, A., *Der sinnhafte Aufbau der sozialen Welt*, Vienna, 1932.

120. Otaka, T., *Grundlegung der Lehre vom sozialen Verband*, Vienna, 1932.

121. Sander, Fritz, *Allgemeine Gesellschaftslehre*, Jena, 1930.

122. Freyer, Hans, *Soziologie als Wirklichkeitswissenschaft, logische Grundlegung des Systems der Soziologie*, Leipzig and Berlin, 1930.

123. Landshut, Siegfried, *Kritik der Soziologie, Freiheit und Gleichheit als Ursprungsproblem der Soziologie*, Berlin, 1929.

124. Halbwachs, Maurice, "Les origines puritaines du capitalisme", in *Revue d'histoire et de philosophie religieuse de l'université de Strasbourg*, March-April, 1929.

125. König, René, *Soziologie heute*, Zürich, 1949.

126. Geiger, Theodor, *Die Klassengesellschaft im Schmelztiegel*, Cologne and The Hague, 1949.

127. Geiger, Theodor, *Aufgaben und Stellung der Intelligenz in der Gesellschaft*, Stuttgart, 1949.

128. Henrich, Dietrich, *Die Einheit der Wissenschaftslehre Max Webers*, Tübingen, 1952.

129. Winckelmann, Johannes, *Legitimität und Legalität in Max Webers Herrschaftssoziologie*, with an Appendix: "Max Weber. Die drei reinen Typen legitimer Herrschaft", Tübingen, 1952.

130. Rüstow, Alexander, "Der Idealtypus oder die Gestalt als Norm", in *Studium Generale*, 1953, No. 1.

FREE PRESS PAPERBACKS

A Series of Paperbound Books in the Social and Natural Sciences, Philosophy, and the Humanities

These books, chosen for their intellectual importance and editorial excellence, are printed on good quality book paper, from the large and readable type of the cloth-bound edition, and are Smyth-sewn for enduring use. Free Press Paperbacks conform in every significant way to the high editorial and production standards maintained in the higher-priced, case-bound books published by The Free Press of Glencoe.

Andrews, Wayne	*Architecture, Ambition, and Americans*	90067
Aron, Raymond	*German Sociology*	90105
Bettelheim, Bruno	*Truants From Life*	90345
Cohen, Morris Raphael	*Reason and Nature*	90609
Coser, Lewis	*The Functions of Social Conflict*	90681
Durkheim, Emile	*The Division of Labor in Society*	90785
Durkheim, Emile	*The Rules of Sociological Method*	90850
Edel, Abraham	*Ethical Judgment*	90890
Eisenstadt, S. N.	*From Generation to Generation*	90938
Evans-Pritchard, E. E.	*Social Anthropology and Other Essays*	90987
Friedmann, Georges	*The Anatomy of Work*	91082
Friedmann, Georges	*Industrial Society*	91090
Geertz, Clifford	*The Religion of Java*	91146
Goode, William J.	*Religion Among the Primitives*	91242
Gouldner, Alvin W.	*Patterns of Industrial Bureaucracy*	91274
Hayek, F. A.	*The Counter-Revolution of Science*	91436
Henry, Andrew F., and James F. Short, Jr.	*Suicide and Homicide*	91442
Janowitz, Morris	*The Professional Soldier*	91618
Katz, Elihu, and Paul F. Lazarsfeld	*Personal Influence*	91715
Lerner, David, and Lucille W. Pevsner	*The Passing of Traditional Society*	91859
Maximoff, G. P.	*The Political Philosphy of Bakunin*	90121
Meyerson, Martin, and Edward C. Banfield	*Politics, Planning and the Public Interest*	92123
Neumann, Franz	*The Democratic and the Authoritarian State*	92291
Park, Robert Ezra	*Race and Culture*	92379
Parsons, Talcott	*Essays in Sociological Theory*	92403
Parsons, Talcott	*The Social System*	92419
Radcliffe-Brown, A. R.	*The Andaman Islanders*	92558
Reiss, Ira L.	*Premarital Sexual Standards in America*	92620
Riesman, David	*Individualism Reconsidered:* UNABRIDGED EDITION	92650
Rosenberg, Bernard, and David Manning White	*Mass Culture: The Popular Arts in America*	92708
Simmel, Georg	*Conflict* AND *The Web of Group Affiliations*	92884
Simmel, Georg	*The Sociology of Georg Simmel*	92892
Sorokin, Pitirim A.	*Social and Cultural Mobility*	93028
Wagner, Philip	*The Human Use of the Earth*	93357
Weber, Max	*The Theory of Social and Economic Organization*	93493

Many of these books are available in their original cloth bindings.
A complete catalogue of all Free Press titles will be sent on request